100 Proofs that the Bible is the Inspired Word of God

And Scientifically Accurate

By Robert Rite

Table of Contents

Get Complimentary Access to: "Prophecy Alerts"

Dear Reader: Prophecies are being fulfilled so rapidly in these last days that I am offering my readers complimentary access to "*prophecy alerts*" so that you get "*Breaking Prophecy News*" as soon as it breaks...Just follow this link below and sign Up today...
http://robertritebooks.com/prophecy-alerts/

Introduction - 100 Proofs and Counting

*"And He said, "**To you it has been given to know the mysteries of the kingdom of God**, but to the rest it is given in parables, that '**Seeing they may not see, and hearing they may not understand**."* **Luke 8:10**

I could have easily listed more than 100 proofs but I felt that 100 was a nice number to stop at. Furthermore, every year more proofs surface as more and more prophecies are fulfilled. It seems that in these last days prophecies are being fulfilled at an accelerated pace.

My book is simply an aid to help build up your faith by offering undeniable proof of the existence of the God of the bible - the God of the universe!

It is my desire that upon reading this book and the many proofs that I have set forth in these pages, that you will develop an unquenchable desire to discover the many truths revealed in the inspired word of God.

The bible is loaded with keys and prophetic codes that can be unlocked once you develop a basic understanding of the principles of truth.

So I challenge you to read this book in its entirety with an unbiased mind so that you can fully understand why these proofs authenticate the accuracy of the ancient prophecies of the scriptures. I am confident that if you read these 100 proofs with an open mind, your eyes will be opened to the truth and you will **no longer** look at the bible as an **old fashioned antiquated book** that is no longer relevant to our modern times.

My objective in writing this book for you is to unlock many ancient prophecies that prove that the Bible is indeed the infallible and inspired word of God. I will cross reference these ancient writings with what is happening today and what modern science has recently discovered - and how they all confirm that the revelations of the bible may indeed reveal divine and supernatural **truths that apply today perhaps even more than at any other time in this age**.

As we embark in an exciting journey through time immemorial, I want to reinforce that I will be noting specific scientific and historic facts that coincide or fulfill writings contained in ancient prophecies.

Upon completing this book I believe that you too will conclude that the Bible is the inspired word of the true living God; full of more wisdom and revelations than a fallen world wants or cares to accept.

Today's world which worships the created more than the creator has been blinded by the forces of this world and cannot understand the truth - but my objective and promise to you is that once you complete this book - your eyes will be opened to these divine truths.

Why it is important to know these Truths

It is very important to get a clear understanding of the truth because I believe that we are getting very close to the time of the end, and it is that moment in time for us to make a decision as to what we believe; our eternal destiny is at stake here.

6

I know this will rattle and upset some, but I know in my heart that the God of Israel and the bible, is the God of the universe, and that there is no other god. We will cover that in a coming section.

Many in these "Modern" times have a really hard time accepting Monotheism (the belief that there is only one God). Fallen man (atheists and alike) will reject these truths even in the midst of the coming apocalypse when it will be clearer more than ever as to who is really in command - the God of the universe. Let's read one of these prophecies:

"Then the **fourth angel** *poured out his bowl on the sun, and power was given to him to scorch men with fire. And men were scorched with great heat, and* **they blasphemed the name of God** *who has power over these plagues;* **and they did not repent and give Him glory**.*"* **Revelation 16:8-9**

Hard to believe, but many will sell their souls to he who has deceived the masses from time immemorial. Yet the devil although limited by the sovereignty of God, can easily deceive the unbeliever because as the **"prince of the power of the air"** one of his main tools is to infiltrate the minds of fallen men so that they believe his lies.

One of his primary lies is that the Bible, Israel, the Jews, Christians and the word are insignificant in these "modern" times. He has also been successful in deluding peoples and nations into believing that Jerusalem does not belong to God or His elect. I believe that God has allowed this as a key test for mankind and the nations, and sadly

7

mankind has fallen for the lie as will be witnessed during the coming tribulation period.

Why so many do NOT believe the Bible is the inspired Word of God?

Many people are quick to shun, reject and doubt the inspired scriptures of the bible. I wager that this is because most of these people have reached conclusions without even reading the bible. Our educational system has failed God and our children by keeping the word and the truth out of the classrooms; yet many cannot understand why schools have become a target for mass murderers and lunatics.

Many reject the scriptures due to preconceived notions based on the opinions of other non-believers and society as a whole. Many others start to read the bible and give up before they can acquire any measurable level of faith and wisdom which are the essential tools to unlock the encrypted messages behind the prophecies.

God wants us to seek Him out and will unlock many secrets once a person starts to read with a measure of faith. In **Luke 8:10** God reveals that those who have no faith in Him or the word will find it somewhat challenging to understand or want to understand the scriptures. Let's read:

*"And He said, "**To you it has been given to know the mysteries of the kingdom of God**, but to the rest it is given in parables, that 'Seeing they may not see, and hearing they may not understand."* **Luke 8:10**

Mathew 13:13-16 - *"Therefore I speak to them in parables, because seeing they do not see, and hearing they do not hear, nor do they understand. And in them the prophecy of Isaiah is fulfilled, which says: 'Hearing you will hear and shall not understand, and seeing you will see and not perceive; for the hearts of this people have grown dull. Their ears are hard of hearing, And their eyes they have closed, Lest they should see with their eyes and hear with their ears, Lest they should understand with their hearts and turn, So that I should heal them. But blessed are your eyes for they see, and your ears for they hear"* (Isaiah **6:9, 10; Is. 58:2; Ps. 78:2)**

As I said earlier, this book cannot save you; only the spirit of truth through the divine **word of God** and the sacrificial blood of the Messiah can save you. Many give up too early in understanding God's messages for mankind. **All you really need** is a solemn desire to know and believe in your creator and seek the truth. Ask God for the wisdom to know the truth and He promises to answer your prayer:

James 1:5 *"If any of you lacks wisdom, let him ask of God who gives to all liberally and without reproach, and it will be given to him."*

"Why does a Merciful God allow such evil in this world?"

We have heard this question time and time again from those experiencing tragedy in their life and also by an unbelieving world. On 9/11 the disbelieving cry was **"*Why do they hate us*"**?

So before we begin, I wanted to address this question because it is one of the reasons that some do not believe, and other have lost faith or rejected God and His word.

We have all endured tragedies in our lives; some are our fault and many are not. But regarding evil, why does God allow it to persist unabated. Well evil comes in many shades of dark; the forces of darkness that permeate this fallen world. We witness rampant iniquity every time we tune into the local and world news. It is hard for many to understand why God allows such evil to persist in this world today. May I suggest a few reasons?

- because of man's iniquity and un-repentance
- because of the curse of original sin
- to test our faith
- because God gave man free will - for each to do as he or she wishes (sadly, some will it to harm others)
- because a person who is suffering a tragedy may be undergoing a time of trial and testing
- because perhaps the afflicted forgot to pray for God's veil of protection
- because God acts in mysterious ways
- because God is allowing time for His children to finally see the light, repent and seek the truth!
- because God reveals that in the last days iniquity will grow exponentially
- because God is waiting for the cup of iniquity to overflow before His hammer drops on the earth
- because God is waiting for the full number of saved

souls to be reached before His hammer drops on the earth

I hope the reasons above can lay that question to rest. A better question is "Why is God so patient"? The answer: because He is so merciful!

So what does all this have to do with the proof of the bible?

Because many fulfilled prophecies relate to things that have happened and are happening today with more frequency and this also proves the ancient prophecies about what will visit us in the perilous times ahead.

The bible is the inspired word of God distributed by 44 inspired writers and prophets over a few thousand years who received these divine words by dictation of the Holy Spirit. This is why all 66 books of the bible, although written by 44 different men, many who did not know each other and lived thousands of years apart, seems to have been written by one person. It all fits like a perfectly completed puzzle. I as well as most bible scholars have yet to discover contradictions - it all fits perfectly! It seems to have been written by one author - because it is. It was written by the inspired word of God!

The French philosopher Voltaire once said that the bible would be obsolete and forgotten, and would become a museum relic within 100 years. Instead, Voltaire was dead in less than fifty years, and the Bible is still the all time best seller.

After Voltaire's death his printing presses were used to print Bibles - Hmmm!

"Heaven and earth shall pass away but my words shall not pass away." **Mathew 24:35**

Chapter 1 - Science, Astronomy, and physics declare the Glory of God

I have shocking news for some; science may not contradict ancient biblical scriptures and prophecies after all. Below are **26 bible prophecies** that science just cannot disprove, and which their theories support or agree with:

Proofs Number 1 to 26

1) Genesis 1:1 - "In the beginning God created the heavens and the earth."
Note: Matter - matters! Since you cannot convert matter to energy, you cannot create energy or matter out of anything - so creation as the bible prophecies establish; is the only possible scenario that makes sense!

2) Genesis 1:26 - Then God said, "let us make man in our own image..."
Note: The fossil record actually supports the bible and bible prophecy which reveals in Genesis 1:26 that man was created last (on the sixth day). The fossil record shows that after man no other new species appear in the fossil record!

3) Genesis 7:4 - "For after seven more days I will cause it to rain on the earth forty days and forty nights, and I will destroy from the face of the earth all living things that I have made."
Note: Science also supports the bible's account of the great flood that may have wiped out all life on earth. 85% of the rock surface around the world is composed of sedimentary rock, indicating that at some time in the past the world was covered by

water. Fossils of fish and other aquatic species have even been discovered on mountain tops, indicating that they ended up there through a worldwide flood.

4) Genesis 1:1 - "In the beginning God created the heavens and the earth"! **Hebrews 11:3** tells us that the universe was framed by the word of God.
Note: Albert Einstein's theory of relativity actually supports that the Universe as well as mass, energy and time all had a beginning, and that some "entity" must have been responsible for its beginning.

5) Isaiah 40:22 - "*It is* He who sits above the circle of the earth, and its inhabitants *are* like grasshoppers; He who stretches out the heavens like a curtain, and spreads them out like a tent to dwell in."
Note: The Bible prophesied thousands of years before science discovered that the Earth was not flat, and that the universe is expanding.

6) Isaiah 34:4 - "All the host of heaven shall be dissolved, and the heavens shall be rolled up like a scroll; all their host shall fall down as the leaf falls from the vine, and as *fruit* falling from a fig tree."
Note: The Second law of Thermodynamics, and Einstein's Theory of Relativity support that the Universe is not eternal; that it had a beginning and will have an end. Einstein's theory showed that the universe is expanding and so it cannot be eternal.

7) Ecclesiastes 1:7 - "All the rivers run into the sea, yet the sea *is* not full; to the place from which the rivers come, there they return again."
Note: Solomon was the third king of Israel not a scientist, yet he was inspired by the Holy Spirit to write the first thesis on condensation and evaporation!

8) Jeremiah 33:22 - As the host of heaven cannot be numbered, nor the sand of the sea measured, so will I multiply the descendants of David My servant and the Levites who minister to Me.'"

Note: God declared that man would never be able to determine how many stars are in the cosmos, and even today with the most advanced telescoping technology astronomers can only make an estimate! They admit that the stars are too numerous to capture and catalog. Astronomers have confirmed what the bible revealed thousands of years ago, that the number of stars in the universe cannot be counted by man. An uncountable number of stars exist in the universe yet our awesome creator has named every single star!

9) Isaiah 40:12 - "Who has measured the waters in the hollow of His hand, Measured heaven with a span And calculated the dust of the earth in a measure? Weighed the mountains in scales and the hills in a balance?"

Note: The size of the Sun and its distance to the earth, the amount of oxygen, and helium in the earth all are perfectly measured so as to support life on earth. It is a very delicate balance. This indicates that the universe and all the creatures in the earth were created and designed by a superior being, not a random, chaotic unorganized event.

Just as the bible and bible prophecy indicate, Science proves that there must be a "force" that holds all the atoms together to keep the perfect balance of hydrogen, helium, oxygen and iron possible. If this force was just 5% weaker then excessive Hydrogen in the air would make life on earth impossible. If 5%

stronger, molecules would all clump together - again making life on earth impossible!
The cosmos is all perfectly balanced by its creator - the God of the Bible; the God of Abraham, Isaac and Jacob. It is He that lives forever and ever!

10) Job 25:5 - "If even **the moon does not shine**, and the stars are not pure in His sight"
Note: For thousands of years men believed that the moon shined on its own, like the sun. Just a century or 2 ago it was finally "discovered" that the moon does not shine, but rather that the moon merely reflects the light of the sun.

11) Job 38:35 - "Can you send out **lightning** that they may go, and say to you, 'Here we *are!*'?"
Note: to the uninitiated this may sound like gibberish - but to me it sounds "electric". I don't know if Ben Franklin may have gotten his idea by reading this passage. But through the path of lightning Ben is credited for advancing the efficient propagation of electricity. Also today through electric currents people can communicate from afar with cell phones, landlines, computers and a host of other devices.

12) Job 26:7 - "He stretches out the north over empty space; *He* hangs the earth on nothing."
Note: Astronomers and physicists have recently determined that the universe is expanding. They could have determined that 2000 years earlier had they studied the ancient scriptures!

13) Job 28:25 - "To establish a weight for the wind, and apportion the waters by measure."
Note: It was not until 1643 that Evangelista Torricelli

invented the barometer under the theory that the air had weight!

14) Job 38:19 "Where *is* **the way *to* the dwelling of light**? And darkness, where *is* its place,"
Note: 3,500 years ago, Job was led to reveal that light travels. Thousands of years later another Jewish man named Albert Einstein established the breakthrough Theory of Relativity based in part on the velocity of light!

15) Psalm 8:8 - "The birds of the air, and the fish of the sea that pass through the paths of the seas."
Note: In the 1800s Mathew Fontaine an Oceanographer, credited Psalm 8:8 as his inspiration to survey and chart the oceanic winds and currents!

16) Isaiah 40:22 - "*It is* He who sits above the circle of the earth, and its inhabitants *are* like grasshoppers, **who stretches out the heavens** like a curtain, and spreads them out like a tent to dwell in."
Note: It took man almost 6,000 years to "discover" that the earth is NOT flat. Yet it was revealed in the Bible over 3,000 years ago! Obviously, the fathers of science also did not read their Bibles ;)

17) Ecclesiastes 1:6 - "The wind goes toward the south, and turns around to the north; the wind whirls about continually, and comes again on its circuit.
Note: the bible was the first to chart the global wind patterns!

18) Leviticus 15:13 - "And when he who has a discharge is cleansed of his discharge, then he shall count for himself seven days for his cleansing, wash his clothes, and bathe his body **in running water**;

then he shall be clean."
Note: The book of Leviticus in the Bible establishes several sanitary and dietary laws which have helped the Jews avoid many of the plagues that struck other civilizations throughout the ages. Today, modern medicine applies many of the hygienic laws that God gave to the Jews thousands of years ago! It was not until the 1800's that Pasteur and Koch published their findings indicating that medical doctors should stop washing their hands in a bowl of water as that would only spread germs and contaminate the patients. From then on doctors were instructed to wash their hands in **running water**!

19) Leviticus 17:11 - "For the life of the flesh is in the blood."
Note: It was revealed thousands of years ago that blood is the life force of the body. Yet for a long time it was actually believed that to cure diseases the blood had to be drained! In fact George Washington died because his blood was drained to mortal levels in an effort to cure an illness!
Modern medicine is so effective today because they understand that the first thing they must do is to stop the bleeding. Blood tests reveal a person's health and help secure a long life through regular examinations.

20) Proverbs 17:22 - A merry heart does good, like medicine, but a broken spirit dries the bones.
Note: It was shocking for mankind to learn recently that laughter is actually good medicine. Yet God revealed this to us in the scriptures thousands of years ago. And of course modern science also confirms how stress and unhappiness harm our health.

Indeed, despite their quest to discredit God as the Creator, even modern science is now making discoveries that actually confirm that the secrets of the universe were declared by God Almighty before He created science, physics and scientists!

21) Scientists claim that we are made from the stars and that without supernova there is no life - that our material all originated from star dust. If that is the case then perhaps that is why Jesus declared that he is the ***bright morning star!*** Indeed, Christ is the star that formed every atom in our body - making us a star child - a child of God!

"Then He brought him outside and said, "Look now toward heaven, and count the stars if you are able to number them." And He said to him, "So shall your descendants be." **Genesis 15:5**

"When the <u>morning stars sang together</u>, and all the sons of God shouted for joy?" **Job 3:9**

"I, Jesus, have sent My angel to testify to you these things in the churches. I am the Root and the Offspring of David, the Bright and Morning Star." **Revelation 22:16**

22) Scientist's claim that as hydrogen dissipates from the universe eventually all stars will disappear. Could that be confirming what God declared thousands of years ago?
*"Now I saw a new heaven and **a <u>new earth, for the first heaven and the first earth had passed away</u>**. Also there was no more sea."* **Revelation 21:1**

23) Scientists claim that sometime in the future the Universe will become totally dark. Could they unknowingly be confirming what the bible declared thousands of years ago:
*"The city had **no need of the sun** or of the moon to shine in it, for the glory of God illuminated it. The Lamb is its light."* **Revelation 21:23**

24) Scientists believe that the future of the universe looks grim per their aforementioned discoveries. There will be no need for astronomy in the new age of God either! Could we become the stars of the new heavens?
***"Those who are wise shall shine like the brightness of the firmament, and those who turn many to righteousness like the stars forever and ever."* Daniel 12:3**

25) If there was a big bang then it must have been God himself who orchestrated it when he said, **let there be light**! A big bang produces light! The universe was once an atom and now it just keeps expanding, just as the body of Christ keeps growing until the full number is reached!
*"I, Jesus, have sent My angel to testify to you these things in the churches. I am the Root and the Offspring of David, the Bright and **Morning Star**."* **Revelation 22:16**

26) Modern Scientists confirm that man is made of dust, just like the stars. How marvelous that not only is man made from dust, but so are the stars, planets and galaxies created from dust. Apparently all matter emanates from dust. This is an astronomical fact - not theory. Fallen man has turned everything to dust, but only God can take dust and create light and life out of it. **In the beginning God created light; Jesus is that light - the light and the life of the world:**

"In the beginning God created the heavens and the earth. The earth was without form, and void; and darkness was on the face of the deep. And the Spirit of God was hovering over the face of the waters. Then God said, "<u>Let there be light and there was light. And God saw the light, that it was good;</u>" Genesis 1:1-3

"Then Jesus spoke to them again, saying, "I am the light of the world. He who follows Me shall not walk in darkness, but have the light of life." John 8:12

Despite how much modern science wants to dispel the prophecies of the bible as a myth, the laws of physics seem to actually confirm many of the bible prophecies foretold thousands of years before the science evolved!
I must rhetorically ask, how could scientific theories and discoveries all align themselves with the word of God? Could all the astronomers and physicists, many who do not believe in God, be consulting their Bibles for a final determination on their scientific theories?

Chapter 2 - Prophecies that Prove Jesus is the Messiah

There are Many Bible Prophecies in The Old Testament That Have all been fulfilled! Many doubters try to dispel the bible prophecies, particularly those of Jesus Christ, claiming that Jesus fulfilled them simply because He and His conspirators were aware of these Old Testament prophecies. Well if that is the case then Jesus is God because he forced many of these Bible prophecies to come to pass (and God did not strike Him dead). Also, many of the fulfilled prophecies were totally out of Jesus control.

For example, how could Christ cause himself to be born in Bethlehem - as prophesied? How could He control being born of the lineage of Abraham and David? How did Jesus control his being spat at or crucified? Or that he was pierced on the side by a centurion, and that none of his bones were broken - as prophesied. How could Jesus control being buried in a Rich man's tomb after his death - as prophesied? Need more proof? No problem! Let's **review several Bible prophecies that prove Christ was indeed the Messiah**.

The following are bible prophecies which foretold that Jesus would be the Messiah:

Proofs Numbers 27 to 72

27. **Isaiah 7:14** - Jesus would be born of a Virgin (Matthew 1:18). The 4 books of the Gospel fulfill this prophesy.

28. **Genesis 49:10** - Jesus would be of the tribe of Judah (Luke 3:23, 33).

29. **Jeremiah 23:5** - Jesus would be of King David's seed (Luke 3:23, 31).

30. **Micah 5:2** - prophesied that the Messiah would be from Bethlehem. **Luke 2:4-6** reveals that Jesus was born in Bethlehem (**Rev. 2:27; Mathew 2:6).**

31. **Deuteronomy 18:18-19** - Jesus would be a prophet (Matthew 21:11).

32. **Psalms 78:2** - prophesied that the Messiah would speak in parables. The 4 Gospels quote many parables from Jesus (Matthew 13:34).

33. **Isaiah 40:3** - Jesus would be preceded by a messenger (Malachi 3:1, and Matthew 3:1-2).

34. **Zechariah 9:9** - *"Rejoice greatly, O daughter of Zion! Shout, O daughter of Jerusalem! Behold, your King is coming to you; he is just and having salvation, Lowly and riding on a donkey, a colt, the foal of a donkey."*
Note: This verse prophesied that the Lord would make his entry into Jerusalem riding on a donkey. In **Luke 19:35-37** we have the account of Jesus entering Jerusalem on a donkey.

35. **Psalms 41:9** - Jesus would be betrayed by a friend (Matthew 26:47-50).

36. **Zechariah 11:12-13** - *"Throw it to the potter"; **that princely price they set on me.** So I took the thirty pieces of silver and threw them into the house of the Lord for the potter."*
Note: This verse prophesied that Jesus would be

betrayed for 30 pieces of silver. This was fulfilled in **Mathew 27:3-10**

37. **Zechariah 13:7** - Jesus would be forsaken by His disciples (Mark 14:50).

38. **Zechariah 11:13** - The money would be thrown in the temple and used to buy the potter's field (Matthew 27:5-7).

39. **Psalms 35:11** - Jesus would be accused by false witnesses (Matthew 26:59-60).

34. **Isaiah 53:7** - Jesus would be silent before His accusers (Matthew 27:12-14).

35. **Isaiah 50:6, 53:5** - Jesus would be beaten by his enemies, and spit in His face. **Mathew 26:67** fulfilled this.
 (Matthew 27:26).

36. **Isaiah 50:6** - Jesus would be spit upon and beaten (Matthew 27:30).

37. **Micah 5:1** - Jesus would be struck in the head with a rod (Matthew 27:30).

38. **Psalms 22:7-8** - Jesus would be mocked (Matthew 27:29, 31).

39. **Psalms 22:16** - The old testament Bible prophesied that the Messiah would be crucified: "they pierced my hands and my feet" (**Psalm 22:16**). Jesus hands and feet would be pierced (Luke 23:33, and John 20:25). Note that this was predicted hundreds of years before the crucifixion was invented.

40. **Psalms 22:18** - here we read that they would gamble for Jesus garments. This was fulfilled in **John 19:23-24**, also **Mathew 27:35** *"Then they crucified Him, and divided His garments, casting lots, that it might be fulfilled which was spoken by the prophet: "They divided My garments among them, and for My clothing they cast lots."* **Psalm 22:18**

41. **Isaiah 53:12** - Jesus would intercede in prayer for His transgressors (Luke 23:34).

42. **Psalms 22:15** - Jesus would suffer thirst (John 19:28).

43. **Psalms 69:21** - prophesied that Jesus would be given vinegar mixed with gall to quench his thirst. This was fulfilled in Mathew 27:34
He would be offered gall and water (Matthew 27:34).

44. **Psalms 22:1** - Jesus would cry, "My God, My God, why hast thou forsaken me!" (Matthew 27:46).

45. **Psalms 89:45** - Jesus would be cut down in His prime (Psalms 89:45 and 102:23-24).

46. **Exodus 12:46** - None of His bones would be broken (Psalms 34:20, and John 19:32-33).

47. **Zechariah 12:10** - They would look upon Him whom they had **pierced** (John 19:34).
Note: To confirm that Jesus had died, a Roman soldier pierced Christ on His side to make sure He was dead. This passage also prophecies that the Jews will feel great remorse and finally accept Christ as their Lord and savior upon His second coming.

48. **Isaiah 53:12** - prophesied that the Messiah would be "numbered with the transgressors. We read in the gospels that Jesus was crucified along with 2 thieves (Matthew 27:38).

49. **Isaiah 53:9** - that Jesus would be buried as a wealthy man. In **Mathew 27:57-60** we learn that Jesus was buried in the tomb of a rich man called Joseph of Arimethia.

50. **Genesis 3:15** - The Old Testament bible prophesied that Jesus would have a natural childbirth, and would come from the seed of a woman (Genesis 3:15), even though he was the son of God. The 4 books of the Gospel, and Galatians 4:4 confirm this.

51. **Isaiah 35:5-6** prophesied that the Messiah would perform many healing miracles. The 4 gospels are full of accounts of healing miracles performed by the Messiah Jesus.

52. King David **prophesied that the Messiah would be rejected by the Jews (Psalm** 118:22). Of course we all know that this happened and Jesus was rejected as the Jewish Messiah.

53. **Psalm 69:4** said that the Messiah would be hated without a reason. This was fulfillment in John 15:25.

54. **Isaiah 65:1** says: *"I was found by those who did not seek Me; I was made manifest to those who did not ask for Me."* **Isaiah 65:1**
Note: Isaiah 65:1 prophesied that although the Jews rejected Messiah, the Gentiles (Christian nations and people) throughout the world would accept Jesus as their Messiah.

55. **Isaiah 11:10 -** *"There shall be a root of Jesse; and He who shall rise to reign over the Gentiles, in Him the Gentiles shall hope."* **Isaiah 11:10**
Note: This is another prophecy from Isaiah confirming that Jesus who would be from the lineage of Jesse, would be the Lord to the Christians - the body of Christ **(Roman's 15:12; Is. 11:1-16 = Zech. 6:12; Mark 1:10; John 3:34; Rev. 12:5)**

56. **Psalm 110:1 -** *"Sit at My right hand till I make your enemies Your footstool."*
Note: This passage as well as **Matt. 22:44** reveals that the Messiah sits at the right hand of God awaiting His second coming (**Rev. 19:11-16**)

57. **Psalm 102:18** - *"This will be written for the generation to come, that a people yet to be created may praise the Lord."* The New Testament books all fulfill this prophecy (Rom. 15:4; 22:31).

58. **Isaiah 53:3, 4, 5, 12** - Isaiah 53 is the catch-all chapter that leaves no doubt as to whom the Messiah is. It describes Christ as one who would be despised and rejected; a man of sorrows wounded for our transgressions; He opened not his mouth; He was numbered with the transgressors. These clearly describe Jesus (also read Ps. 22:6; John 1:10, 11; Matt 8:17; Matt 26:63)

59. **Hosea 11:1** *"Out of Egypt I called my son"*
Note: - Joseph and Mary fled to Egypt to hide Jesus from Herod who wanted to kill him as he believed the child would be a threat to his kingdom. And they returned from Egypt once the threat was over **(Matthew 2:16).**

60. **Haggai 2:9** - "The glory of this latter temple shall be greater than the former,' says the Lord of hosts. 'And in this place I will give peace,' says the Lord of hosts."
Note: This is because the later temple would be the one that Jesus Christ visited while He was on earth.

61. **Is. 49:5-6 -** *"And now the Lord says, who formed Me from the womb to be His Servant, to bring Jacob back to Him, so that Israel is gathered to Him (For I shall be glorious in the eyes of the Lord, and My God shall be My strength). Indeed He says, 'it is too small a thing that You should be My Servant to raise up the tribes of Jacob, and to restore the preserved ones of Israel;* **I will also give You as a light to the Gentiles, that You should be My salvation to the ends of the earth".** **42:6; 51:4 = Matt 23:37; Luke 2:32; Acts 13:47**
Note: Jesus, a descendant of the Jews became savior to the world.

62. **Dan. 9:26** - *"And after the sixty-two weeks Messiah shall be cut off, but not for Himself; and the people of the prince who is to come shall destroy the city and the sanctuary. The end of it shall be with a flood, and till the end of the war desolations are determined".* **Matt. 27:50**
Note: this prophecy was fulfilled with the death of Jesus.

63. **Dan. 12:5-6** - As Daniel's vision is ending, we are taken to the very end of time where the man in linen (Jesus Christ) appears, just like He will at the very end of time (**Rev. 19:11-16**)!

Above are just some of the fulfilled prophecies on the Messiah. Indeed, Jesus fulfilled 109 Old Testament prophesies.

Chapter 3 - the Jewish Feast Days point to Jesus as Messiah

Proof # 64 to 72

Many Christians (and Jews of course) have no idea that the Jewish feast days are yet another revelation of how Jesus was indeed the coming and soon returning Messiah!

The good news is that these truths will be revealed to the Jews as God opens their eyes in these last days (**read Zechariah 12:10; 14:16-19; Isaiah 66:7-14; Romans 11:11; Romans 11:26**). This has been prophesied in various places in the bible. In the last days before the return of the Lord, millions of Jews will convert to Messianic Jews (Jews who accept Jesus Christ as the Messiah).

Many Jews have been blinded by their misguided beliefs, doctrines, and their Rabbis into believing that they cannot be a Jew and believe in Jesus. As a result they have postponed many blessings and have received repeated trials, persecution and curses over the past 1900 years.
Let's review each appointed feast day and how each feast day is actually identifying Jesus as the Messiah.

Proof 64 - Passover (Pesach):
There is no clearer feast day that commemorates Jesus as the Lamb of God that takes away the sins of the world. Passover feast is an 8 day period that also includes the feast of unleavened bread and first fruits which are also covered below.

- To the Jews this day celebrates their deliverance

from Egyptian slavery.
- To the Christian this day should celebrate our deliverance from the bondage (slavery) from sin.
- The Passover Lamb must be a male with no blemishes (no sin). Jesus was a male and never sinned. In John 1:29 we learn that Jesus is the Lamb of God that takes away the sins of the world.
- The blood on the doorpost, and the breaking of the bread are symbolic of Jesus blood and body, as he gave both of them up at the cross, so that we too could become blameless (with no blemishes/sin).
- Psalm 118:22, Matthew 21:42, 1 Peter 2:7 all teach that Jesus would be rejected (he was crucified during the Passover feast)
- The last supper commemorates the sacrifice of Jesus as the perfect lamb (Isaiah 53, Luke 22:20; 1 Corinthians 5:7; Ephesians 2:11-13)

Proof 65 - Feast of Unleavened Bread (Hag HaMatzot): (starts at sundown one day after Passover)

Unleavened bread is eaten during this 8 day feast (including Passover) as a symbol of purity since it contains no leaven which symbolizes sin (**1 Corinthians 5:7-8**). Jesus, who lived a perfect sinless life, was the "bread of life" who came down from heaven, providing the living bread so that he who eats of this bread will never die (**John 6:32, 35, 41 and 48**).

- The unleavened bread is striped and pierced during baking, just as Jesus was ("by his stripes we are healed" **Isaiah 53:5**)!

Proof 66 - First Fruits (Reishit):

This feast day celebrates the "manna" (food) that God rained down to the Israelites during their 40 years in the wilderness. This Jewish feast is celebrated on the third day of Passover.

Jesus, the bread who came down from heaven (symbolic of manna), was resurrected from the dead on the 3rd day as well (**Luke 24:44-47**).

- Jesus is the "first fruit" of many future resurrections to come when he returns. Christians celebrate Jesus resurrection during Easter.
- Interesting how only 3 items were placed inside the **Ark of the Covenant (symbolic of the throne in heaven**). **One of them was "manna".**
Jesus (which Manna symbolized), today sits at the right hand of God in His heavenly throne!

Proof 67 - Feast of Weeks (Shavuot - Pentecost):

Occurs 50 days after Passover in celebration of the Lords blessing of the summer harvest. The Ten Commandments are also celebrated at this feast, as they are believed to have been given during this time.

- Christians celebrate this period in time as **Pentecost**. Around 50 days after the Passover (the week during which Jesus was resurrected to heaven). This is the day that the **Holy Spirit** was first introduced to the early Christian believers - recognized today as **Pentecost (Joel 2:28-32; Acts 2:32-33; Acts 2:41; Jeremiah 31:31; Hebrews 9:14-15**)

Proof 68 - Rosh Hashanah (Feast of Trumpets):

These are the Jewish **High Holy Feast days** - and constitute a 10 day period ending on **Yom Kippur (day of Atonement)**. This feast period is sometimes also referred to as the Days of repentance. The shofar (ram's horn) is blown 100 times during the synagogue services. It is a period of repentance so that their names remain or are replaced into the **"Book of Life"**.

- We Christians also believe in the **Book of Life**. In **Revelation 21:27** it is referred to as the **"Lamb's book of life"**, and <u>**the only way to have our name "permanently" inscribed in it is through our faith and proclamation of Jesus Christ as Lord and savior (John 10:27-30).**</u> We too must repent so that our name is written in the book of life and so we are not subject to judgment day (Revelation 20:15).

Proof 69 - Yom Kippur (Day of Atonement):

This is the most **solemn Holy day** of the Jewish calendar. It is symbolic of the final Day of Judgment when God judges the people. In Old Testament times it was a time of fasting and prayer, and the **high priest** would sacrifice an animal to pay for the sins of the people (read **Leviticus 16:8-10; 20-22; 29-34)**.

- The **Holy of Holies** (symbolic of Heaven) was separated from the people via a thick veil and could only be entered once a year on **Yom Kippur** by the high priest, when he entered to offer the **blood sacrifice of atonement** on behalf of the Jewish people.

- Since the Jews rejected Jesus as Messiah, once the temple was destroyed around A.D. 70, they were left unable to atone for their sins via the traditional temple sacrifice. So instead of recognizing that Jesus was indeed the Messiah they had been praying for, they now substituted temple sacrifices with a new tradition of prayer and other good works to atone for their sins.

- When Jesus died for our sins, **the veil** (symbolic of separation from sin) **was ripped from top to bottom (Luke 23:44-46).** Christ **became our High Priest** and through his blood he paid the atonement for all of our sins, once and for all - so that all who believe will not perish but enjoy eternal life (**Hebrews 9:11-28; Romans 3:21-25)!**

Proof 70 - Feast of Tabernacle (Sukkot - Feast of Booths):

This feast period commemorates how the Jewish people lived under God's care and faithful protection for 40 years in the wilderness. During this time they live in makeshift booths, since during the 40 years in the wilderness of journey they lived in booths (temporary tents made of branches).

- This feast consists of several ceremonies fulfilled by and symbolic of Jesus.
- The Golden Lamp stands indicate that the Messiah would be a light to the Gentiles (**Isaiah 49:6**). Jesus said in **John 8:12** "I am the light of the world".
- The water from the pool of Siloam to the temple, also symbolizes that when the Messiah comes (Jesus also called Jeshua) the whole earth will know God as

the waters cover the sea (**Isaiah 11:9; John 7:37-38**)

- Just as God led the Jews out of the wilderness (sin and sorrows) and into the promised land, Jesus came to lead us out of sin and to paradise.

Proof 71 - Hanukkah (Feast of Dedication):

Celebrates the Maccabees victory over the Greeks, and the subsequent cleansing and rededication of the temple in 165 BC after Antiochus Epiphanes (a satanically controlled person, who was also representative of the coming antichrist) defiled the temple. It also celebrates the miracle of the flame that burned for the 8 days despite provisions of oil for just one day.

- To us Christians the **Feast of Dedication** (which is celebrated in early winter) is symbolic of our **Christmas celebration**, whereby we celebrate **the birth of our savior the Messiah Jesus**, despite the fact that Herod (a form of antichrist) tried to have him murdered along with all babies born in his town. Jesus birth, and subsequent ministry, death, resurrection, and return has already defeated Satan and the antichrist even though they once again will try to defile the rebuilt temple in the last days - just before Jesus triumphant return to establish Messianic rule on earth (read **Daniel 11:31** and **Revelation 19:11-21**).

Proof 72 - Purim (Feast of Lots):

Celebrates the preservation of the Jewish people through the Jewish Queen Esther during their exile in Persia (current day Iran).

- This **last** of the feast days is just as symbolic of Jesus the Messiah as the **first** (Passover). **Queen Esther** (symbolic of the Church) was able to foil **Haman's (symbolic of Satan** and the **Antichrist**) plot to massacre all of the Jewish people. Her adopted father **Mordecai (symbolic of the Messi**ah Jesus) convinced her to remain faithful to her Jewish heritage, and courageously stand up against the evil plot of Haman at the risk of her own persecution (Read the **book of Esther, and Esther 4:13-14**)

It is time for Gentiles (Christians) and Jews to unite together so that we can complete the mission that God called us to complete. Only then can we enjoy the fullness of God and Jesus on earth. We must share these insights with our fellow brethren and our Jewish brothers. Doing so will be a great blessing to us all, as we fulfill God's word and command that we be the light of the world (Mathew 5:14-16).

Note: the dates of these feast days vary slightly from year to year; so just research them online).

Chapter 4 - Fulfilled Prophecies on Israel that prove the Accuracy of the Bible

Proof # 73 - That the Jews would be scattered Among the Nations and persecuted

Jesus prophesied of the destruction of the temple and Jerusalem which occurred in 70 AD

Matthew 23:37-39 - *"O Jerusalem, Jerusalem, the one who kills the prophets and stones those who are sent to her! How often I wanted to gather your children together, as a hen gathers her chicks under her wings, but you were not willing! See! Your house is left to you desolate; 39 for I say to you, you shall see Me no more till you say, 'Blessed is He who comes in the name of the Lord!"*

There were many prophecies that foretold the Israelites would be scattered out of Israel. After 70 AD the whole land became desolate for over 1800 years. They endured much persecution and the holocaust during their judgment.

Matthew 24:1-2 - *"Then Jesus went out and departed from the temple, and His disciples came up to show Him the buildings of the temple. And Jesus said to them, "Do you not see all these things? Assuredly, I say to you, **not one stone shall be left here upon another, that shall not be thrown down**."*

Leviticus 26:33 - I will scatter you among the nations and draw out a sword after you; your land shall be desolate and your cities waste.

Ezekiel 12:15 - "Then they shall know that I *am* the Lord, when I scatter them among the nations and disperse them throughout the countries."

Deut 28:64-66 - "Then the Lord will scatter you among all peoples, from one end of the earth to the other, and there you shall serve other gods, which neither you nor your fathers have known—wood and stone. And among those nations you shall find no rest, nor shall the sole of your foot have a resting place; but there the Lord will give you a trembling heart, failing eyes, and anguish of soul. Your life shall hang in doubt before you; you shall fear day and night, and have no assurance of life."

Deut. 4:27-28 (Deut. 28:64) - *"And the Lord will scatter you among the peoples, and you will be left few in number among the nations where the Lord will drive you. And there you will serve gods, the work of men's hands, wood and stone, which neither see nor hear nor eat nor smell."*

There are many prophecies which foretold that Israel would be scattered among the nations - which occurred in 70 AD and lasted approximately 1900 years.

Psalm 83:1-18 is a psalm not just about the nations coming after Israel in the last days, but it has already been partly fulfilled given the rhetoric and threats from Israel's neighbors who regularly call for wiping Israel off the face of the earth, and chanting death to Israel, while burning their flag. Let's read verse four:

Psalm 83:4 - They have said, "Come, and let us cut them off from being a nation, that the name of Israel may be remembered no more."

That Jesus would be Martyred

Dan. 9:26 - *"And after the sixty-two weeks Messiah shall be cut off, but not for Himself; and the people of the prince who is to come shall destroy the city and the sanctuary. The end of it shall be with a flood, and till the end of the war desolations are determined.* **Matt. 27:50; Luke 19:43, 44**

That Israel would hinder world peace

It was prophesied thousands of years ago that Jerusalem would become a **"burdensome stone"** to all the nations. Today, not a day passes by that we do not hear of turmoil in the Middle East and threats and conflicts surrounding Jerusalem. It seems like the three major religions, and all of Israel's neighbors want control of the Holy city at any cost. (Read **Zechariah 12:2-3)**

Proof # 74 - That Israel would be reborn as a sovereign Nation

The following are prophecies that Israel would be re-gathered to their land from the four corners of the earth were fulfilled in 1948:

Ezekiel 37:21 - *"Then say to them, 'thus says the Lord God: "Surely I will take the children of Israel from among the nations, wherever they have gone, and will gather them from every side and bring them into their own land."*

Is. 11:12 - *"He will set up a banner for the nations, and will assemble the outcasts of Israel, and gather together the dispersed of Judah from the four corners of the earth."*

The Lord foretold this future rebirth thousands of years ago, during the time of Moses!

"The Lord will restore you from captivity, and have compassion on you, and will gather you again from all the peoples where the Lord your God has scattered you. If your outcasts are at the ends of the earth, from there the Lord your God will gather you, and from there He will bring you back. And the Lord your God will bring you into the land which your fathers possessed, and you shall possess it" (**Deuteronomy 30:3-5**).

Proof # 75 - That Israel would recapture Jerusalem

This prophecy was fulfilled in 1967, when Israel recaptured the entire city. "They will fall by the sword and will be taken as prisoners to all the nations. Jerusalem will be trampled on by the Gentiles until the times of the Gentiles are fulfilled." **Luke 21:24**

Note: This had to happen since the end time prophecies clearly reveal that the Messiah will establish His kingdom in a revamped "**New Jerusalem**" (**Revelation 21**).
Also, the third temple will be rebuilt in the area of Mount Mariah (Jerusalem) at the time of the end: **Ezekiel 43:1-4**

Proof # 76 - That knowledge would Increase at the Time of the end

The prophet Daniel prophesied thousands of years ago that in the last days knowledge would increase exponentially. With the advent of the Internet, search engines, Web 2.0 social platforms, and smart phones, information is readily available, and anyone can learn anything instantly in direct fulfillment of the Daniel's prophecy over 2,500 years ago.

Daniel 12:4 - *"But you, Daniel, shut up the words, and seal the book until the time of the end; **many shall run to and fro, and knowledge shall increase**."*

Proof # 77 - That there will be an increase in Earthquakes and other Natural Phenomenon

Jesus prophesied that in the last days there would be an increase in the intensity of Earthquakes. The recent 9.0 earthquake in Japan brings the total of 8.0 or higher earthquakes to 6 over the past 60 or so years. We are now averaging over 600 major earthquakes (over 6.5 in the Richter scale) per decade - more than any other time in history

Mathew 24:7 - *"For nation will rise against nation, and kingdom against kingdom. And there will be famines, pestilences, and **earthquakes in various places**."*

Proof # 78 - That Christians and Jews will be hated in the last days
Christ prophesied that in the last days Christians will be hated. They are not only hated by some but mocked, shunned and ridiculed by many. No proof needed here!

41

Mathew 24:9 *"Then they will deliver you up to tribulation and kill you, and you will be hated by all nations for My name's sake."*

That there will be a falling away from the church

The apostle Paul prophesied that in the last days there will be an apostasy (a falling away) whereby many Christian churches will grow cold. Surveys performed over the past 20 years show that the vast majority of prophesying Christians do **NOT believe that the Bible** is the inspired, inerrant word of God.

1 Timothy 4:1 - *"Now the Spirit expressly says that in latter times some will depart from the faith, giving heed to deceiving spirits and doctrines of demons,"*

In **2 Timothy 3:2** Paul prophesied that in the last days men will become lovers of their own selves. Today, society is driven by several doctrines of self-love such as the "human potential movement", and false doctrines that we are gods. The norm today in public schools is to teach the youth that self love and self esteem is the cornerstone to success. No mention of God or the bible, humility or love towards others!

2 Timothy 3:2 - *"For men will be lovers of themselves, lovers of money, boasters, proud, blasphemers, disobedient to parents, unthankful, unholy,"*

Chapter 5 - Holocaust and 9/11 Prophecies

Proof # 79

The following passages may be prophecies related to the Nazi Holocaust. Many Jews were cremated in Auschwitz and other death camps.

Ez. 21:32 *"You **shall be fuel for the fire**; your blood shall be in the midst of the land. You shall not be remembered, for I the Lord have spoken."*

Ez. 23:26; Ex. 34:14; Is. 3:18-23 - *"They shall take your sons and daughter devoured by fire, they will strip her of her clothes and take away her Jewelry."*

Ez.37:1-6 - *"The hand of the Lord came upon me and brought me out in the Spirit of the Lord, and set me down in the midst of the valley; and it was full of bones. Then He caused me to pass by them all around, and behold, there were very many in the open valley; and indeed they were very dry. And He said to me, "Son of man, can these bones live?" So I answered, "O Lord God, You know." Again He said to me, "Prophesy to these bones, and say to them, 'O dry bones, hear the word of the Lord! Thus says the Lord God to these bones: "Surely I will cause breath to enter into you, and you shall live. I will put sinews on you and bring flesh upon you, cover you with skin and put breath in you; and you shall live. Then you shall know that I am the Lord".*

Jer. 9:16 *"I will scatter them also among the Gentiles, whom neither they nor their fathers have* *known. And I will send a sword after them **until I have consumed them**."*

Deut 28:62 - *"You shall be left few in number, whereas you were as the stars of heaven in multitude, because you would not obey the voice of the Lord your God."*

Psalm 44:22 (Rom. 8:36) - As it is written: "For Your sake we are killed all day long; **we are accounted as sheep for the slaughter**."

Proof # 80 - Prophecies on 9/11

We must understand that prophecies in the scriptures are sometimes dual in nature, meaning that they may apply to different nations at different times throughout this age. So when we read the passages below, keep in mind that while they may have applied to Ephraim (who some believe refers to modern day America), they also apply to any other nation through time where the prophecies fit. Understand that this has to be the case since almost none of the western nations, nor Middle East nations existed at least by modern name at the time these prophecies were penned.

Isaiah 9:9-11 *"All the people will know - Ephraim and the inhabitant of Samaria - Who say in pride and arrogance of heart:*

"The bricks have fallen down, but we will rebuild with hewn stones; the sycamores are cut down, but we will replace them with cedars."
Therefore the Lord shall set up the adversaries of Rezin against him, and spur his enemies on"

44

Note: Even the numbers of the verse above includes 9/11! Although the towers fell, America proudly declared that the tower would be rebuilt. They were rebuilt just as prophesied in verses 9-11.

Is. 10:33 "with **terror** He will hew down those of high stature."
Note: Could this be referring to the Twin towers which collapsed during the 9/11 "**terror**" attacks.

Amos 2:9 *"Yet it was I who destroyed the Amorite before them, whose height was like the height of the cedars, and he was as strong as the oaks; yet I destroyed his fruit above and his roots beneath."*

Is. 33:18-19 - *"Your heart will **meditate on terror**: "Where is the scribe?*
*Where is he who weighs? Where is he who **counts the towers**?" You will not see a fierce people, a people of obscure speech, beyond perception, of a stammering tongue that you cannot understand.*
Note: This passage is another clue since **terrorist factions did seek out and destroy the twin towers.**

Isaiah 30:25 *"There will be on every high mountain And on every high hill Rivers and streams of waters, In the day of the great slaughter, When the **towers fall**."*

Chapter 6 - End Time Prophecies That Have Already been fulfilled

Proof # 81

These are just a few of the end time prophecies that have already been fulfilled and there are many more:

Jer. 9:11 (and Is. 25:2) prophesied that Jerusalem would be destroyed; which occurred in 70 AD.

Jer. 9:16 *"I will **scatter them also among the Gentiles**, whom neither they nor their fathers have known. And I will send a sword after them until I have consumed them."* (also read **Lev. 26:33)**

Note: after 70 AD the Jews were scattered throughout the world, and they occupy areas that were not known by their fathers at the time the prophecies were written - because those nations did not exist at the time.

Ez. 11:17-19 - God once again promised through Ezekiel that He would gather them from the nations and bring them back to Israel (see also **Jer. 3:12, 18; 32, 39)**

Ez. 36:19 (also Ez. 22-27; Deut 28:64; Rom. 2:24; Ps. 106:8) - are prophecies that God who scattered Israel among all the nations, will bring her back to her land - not because of the Jews sake, for they profaned His name in their midst, but for God's Holy name's sake. This was fulfilled in 1948.

Ez. 36:34-35 Joel 2:3 - *"The desolate land shall be tilled instead of lying desolate in the sight of all who* pass by. So they will say, '***This land that was desolate has become like the garden of Eden***; and ***the wasted, desolate, and ruined cities are now fortified and inhabited***." (also read **Joel 2:3**) **Ezekiel 36:29-30** "*...**I will call for the grain and multiply it***, and bring no famine upon you. 30 And **I will multiply the fruit of your trees and the increase of your fields,** so that you need never again bear the reproach of famine among the nations.*"

Note: After Israel was destroyed in the first century AD, the land became desolate and undesired. After 1948 when Israel was reborn as a nation the land has become extremely productive and certain parts of Israel (the farm land areas) are so fertile today that these areas can be likened to the **Garden of Eden**.

Ez. 37:19 = Zech 10:6 - "*say to them, 'Thus says the Lord God: "**Surely I will take the stick of Joseph, which is in the hand of Ephraim**, **and the tribes of Israel, his companions**; and **I will join them with it, with the stick of Judah, and make them one stick, and they will be one in My hand**.*"
Note: Today after 1948, the nations of Judah, and Israel are once again united.

Joel 3:1-2 - "*For behold, in those days and at that time, when I bring back the captives of Judah and Jerusalem, I will also gather all nations, and bring them down to the Valley of Jehoshaphat; and I will enter into judgment with them there on account of My people, **My heritage Israel, whom they have scattered among the nations; they have also divided up My land**.*" **Jer. 30:3; Zech 14:2**

Note: This is another fulfilled prophecy whereby the nations are "hell bent" on dividing up God's holy land. This passage also reveals that this is why God will judge all nations at the time of the end.

Mathew 23:37-39 - In this verse Jesus prophesied Israel's destruction in 70 AD because they rejected Him as their Messiah; they did not recognize their Messiah on the day of His visitation:

"O Jerusalem, Jerusalem, the one who kills the prophets and stones those who are sent to her! How often I wanted to gather your children together, as a hen gathers her chicks under her wings, but you were not willing! See! Your house is left to you desolate; for I say to you, you shall see Me no more till you say, 'Blessed is He who comes in the name of the Lord!'

Matthew 21:33-45 "Hear another parable: There was a certain landowner who planted a vineyard and set a hedge around it, dug a winepress in it and built a tower. And he leased it to vinedressers and went into a far country. Now when vintage-time drew near, he sent his servants to the vinedressers, that they might receive its fruit. And the vinedressers took his servants, beat one, killed one, and stoned another. Again he sent other servants, more than the first, and they did likewise to them. Then last of all he sent his son to them, saying, 'They will respect my son.' But when the vinedressers saw the son, they said among themselves, '**This is the heir. Come, let us kill him and seize his inheritance.**' So they took him and cast him out of the vineyard and killed him.

"Therefore, when the owner of the vineyard comes, what will he do to those vinedressers?"

They said to Him, "He will destroy those wicked men miserably, **and lease his vineyard to other vinedressers who will render to him the fruits in their seasons.**"

Jesus said to them, "Have you never read in the Scriptures:
'The stone which the builders rejected has become the chief cornerstone.
This was the Lord's doing, and it is marvelous in our eyes'?

"**_Therefore I say to you, the kingdom of God will be taken from you and given to a nation bearing the fruits of it._** And whoever falls on this stone will be broken; but on whomever it falls, it will grind him to powder."
Note: This parable prophesied how the gentiles (Christian nations and people) would be those who would embrace Jesus message and accept Him as their Messiah, and thus would eventually spread the gospel message throughout the world. The "nation" referred to here could be pointing to America since it was and is the Christian nation that has sent more missionaries throughout the world than any other nation (127,000 out of 400,000 missionaries were sent by America throughout the world in just 2010 - **source**: Huffington Post).

This is the key revelation of **Matthew 21:43**
"Therefore I say to you, the kingdom of God will be taken from you (the Jews) and given to a

nation bearing the fruits of it (USA/Christian Nations). Emphasis and annotations are mine.

God in His mercy and because He always keeps His word, had to bring the Jews back into their homeland, as God had promised to Abraham that the land of Israel would be given to his descendants as an everlasting covenant. So he brought them back not because the Jews repented, but for Gad's Holy name sake. Let's read:

 "Therefore say to the house of Israel, 'thus says the Lord God: "I do not do this for your sake, O house of Israel, but for My holy name's sake, which you have profaned among the nations wherever you went. And I will sanctify My great name, which has been profaned among the nations, which you have profaned in their midst; and the nations shall know that I am the Lord," says the Lord God, "when I am hallowed in you before their eyes." **Isaiah 36:22-23**

One of the key prophecies that trigger the time of the end was when Israel was reborn as a nation fulfilling many end time prophecies such as the following: **Isaiah 36:24** - *"For I will take you from among the nations, gather you out of all countries, and bring you into your own land."*

That heaven and earth would pass away but His word will not. The bible and Christians have withstood thousands of years of persecution and laws banning its use - and it remains the number one best seller in the history of mankind!

Mathew 24:35: That heavens and the earth would pass away but His word will not. The bible and

Christians have withstood thousands of years of persecution and laws banning its use - and it remains the number one best seller in the history of mankind!

Proof # 82 - That the Gentile Nations would inherit the Priesthood of the Lord which the Jews rejected

- **Numbers 14:21-22** *"but truly, as I live, **all the earth shall be filled with the glory of the Lord**— because all these men who have seen My glory and the signs which I did in Egypt and in the wilderness, and have put Me to the test now these ten times, and have not heeded My voice"*.

Note: This verse assured us that the whole world would eventually receive the right to become priests of God and Jesus because of the Israelite's rebellion against God in the wilderness.

Below, God reveals to Moses that upon Moses death that the Israelites would go after other gods after they would inherit the promised land. This is why the torch of the priesthood was passed on to the body of Christ - the Christian nations and people.

"And the Lord said to Moses: "Behold, you will rest with your fathers; and this people will rise and play the harlot with the gods of the foreigners of the land, where they go to be among them, and they will forsake Me and break My covenant which I have made with them.
Then My anger shall be aroused against them in that day, and I will forsake them, and I will hide My face from them, and they shall be devoured. And many evils and troubles shall befall them, so that they will

say in that day, 'Have not these evils come upon us because our God is not among us?'
And I will surely hide My face in that day because of all the evil which they have done, in that they have turned to other gods." **Deut. 31:16-18**

Isaiah 11:10 "And in that day there shall be a Root of Jesse, who shall stand as a banner to the people; for the **Gentiles shall seek Him**, and His resting place shall be glorious."

Note: this verse speaks of the Messiah Jesus, who would come and would be accepted by 2 billion Gentiles (Christians) as the Messiah.

Chapter 7 - Prophecies that Reveal the future and the end of this Age!

Proof # 83

No other divine book contains such detailed prophecies and revelations of what the future holds than the Holy Bible.

Let's review some of the key prophecies that reveal the things that are to come in the near future and during the apocalypse (also referred to as the great tribulation, time of Jacob's troubles, day of the Lord, day of the Lord's wrath, day of the Lord's anger, etc.). There are many more but these are just a few of the key ones:

Joel 1:15 *"Alas for the day; for the day of the Lord is at hand; it shall come as destruction from the Almighty."* **(Jer. 30:7; Joel 2:1)**

Note: The day of the Lord is referred to as the apocalypse and tribulation period. It is the coming seven years of the time of the end, when Satan and those under his possession will try to unite the world against God and destroy His elect!

Joel 2:1 - Blow the trumpet in Zion, and sound an alarm in My holy mountain! Let all the inhabitants of the land tremble; for the day of the Lord is coming, for it is at hand."
Note: I believe that the day of the Lord is at hand today.
As the following passage indicates, at the time of the end, apparently most will have abandoned the God of the bible and or bibles will be made illegal; not just in

certain regions but throughout the world. Also, the Lord will remove His Holy Spirit from the world during the apocalypse - He will have turned His back on a fallen world that has rejected Him **(also read Ezek. 7:26; Hos. 5:6)**.

Amos 8:11-12 - *"Behold, the days are coming," says the Lord God, that I will send a famine on the land, not a famine of bread, nor a thirst for water, but of hearing the words of the Lord. They shall wander from sea to sea, and from north to east; they shall run to and fro, seeking the word of the Lord, but shall not find it."*

That There will be an increase in Violence

In **Mathew 24:37** Jesus warned that as in the days of Noah, the last days will be full of violence. Just watch the evening news and you will be bombarded with so much news on violent acts, so as to depress most anyone. The FBI forecasts show that violent crimes have increased over 500% in the USA since 1960.

Knowledge will Increase Exponentially just before the time of the end

- **Daniel 12:4** *"But you, Daniel, shut up the words, and seal the book **until the time of the end**; many shall run to and fro, and knowledge shall increase."*

The following prophecy has already been fulfilled. As we can see before our eye, in these end times technology has allowed knowledge to increase exponentially as information is available in milliseconds. Computing power has been doubling every 18 to 24 months. In fact the computing power of today's personal computers far exceeds the computing power of the Cray computers of the 1950's! Today's search engines allow anyone to obtain instant information and knowledge on just about any topic.

The Jews will Eventually recognize Christ as their Messiah

The following passages prophecy that at the time of the end the Jews will finally accept Christ as their long awaited Messiah. This realization will probably occur to them at the end of this age, most likely during the seven year tribulation period.

Zechariah 12:10 *"And I will pour on the house of David and on the inhabitants of Jerusalem the Spirit of grace and supplication; then* **they will look on Me whom they pierced**. *Yes,* **they will mourn for Him** *as one mourns for his only son, and grieve for Him as one grieves for a first born."*

Jeremiah 24:7 *"Then I* **will** *give them a heart to* **know** *Me, that I am the Lord; and* **they** *shall be My people, and I* **will** *be their God, for* **they** *shall return to Me with their whole heart."*

Many Shall Perish during the Apocalypse

In the passages below Jesus alerts us that unless the Lord returns during the apocalypse at the time that He will, then no flesh would be saved; but for the elect's sake, whom He chose, He shortened the days. This clearly warns of how bad things will get.

Mark 13:20 *"And unless the Lord had shortened those days, no flesh would be saved; but for the elect's sake, whom He chose, He shortened the days."*

Isaiah 24:5-6
"The earth is polluted because of its inhabitants, **because they have transgressed the laws, violated the statutes, and broken the everlasting covenant.** *Therefore the curse has devoured the earth, and those who dwell in it are desolate. Therefore the inhabitants of the earth are burned, and few men are left."* (also read **Isaiah 66:15-16; Rev. 19:12; Rev. 19:15)**
God will be the one who exacts Judgment upon the Earth

It is clear that God first judged Israel as an example for the world because of her iniquity and rejection of the Lord. So the judgment started with Israel as the example for the world, but the judgments will soon spread to all the nations of the earth for the same reasons. When God removes His veil of protection from all the nations, this is when the apocalypse begins.

On the day of God's wrath **God will declare war upon all the nations**. This is re-confirmed in the following verses:

Is. 25:7 - "And He will destroy on this mountain the surface of the covering cast over all people, and the veil that is spread over **_all nations_**."

Is. 34:2 - the indignation of the Lord is **_against all nations_**, and their armies **(read also Joel 2:20; Rev. 6:14)**.

Jer. 25:15 - Take the wine cup of fury from My hand, and cause **_all the nations_** to whom I send you to drink it. This will become a sword against all the nations; all inhabitants of the earth.

Obadiah 1:15 - "For the day of the Lord upon all the nations is near; as you have done, it shall be done to you; your reprisal shall return upon your own head."

Joel 3:9 - "Proclaim this among the nations: "Prepare for war! Wake up the mighty men, let all the men of war draw near, let them come up."

Joel 3:12 - _"Let the nations be wakened, and come up to the Valley of Jehoshaphat; for there **I will sit to judge all the surrounding nations**."_
The "**valley of decision**" will be the battle of Armageddon when the Messiah annihilates all the nations that come after Israel. This is a pivotal moment for all the nations to finally know and admit that the God of Israel is the Lord of the world - and **they will have to make a decision between the lion who devours the souls of men (Satan) and the Lion of the Tribe of Judah (Messiah Jesus).**

Joel 3:14 *"Multitudes, multitudes in the **valley of decision**! For the day of the Lord is near in the **valley of decision**."*

The coming Day of the Lord (the Great Tribulation) will be upon all the nations. It is also referred to as the times of the Gentiles (**Ezek. 30:3).**

Zephaniah 2:11 - "For He will reduce to nothing **all the gods of the earth**; p*eople* shall worship Him, each one from his place, indeed **all the shores of the nations**." **(also read Mal. 1:11)**

Psalm 75:10 - reveals that God will destroy all the wicked nations, and exalt the righteous ones.

Then they will know who is the Lord

The main reason for God's judgments is so that as many souls as possible will repent and be saved before the end of this age. He wants the world to finally know who the Lord is.

Ezekiel 6:14 *"So I will stretch out My hand against them and make the land desolate, yes, more desolate than the wilderness toward Diblah, in all their dwelling places. Then they shall know that I am the Lord."*

Apparently even the non-believers and those who reject God's word will know that **God is the one judging the earth** during the apocalypse because the bible reveals that the inhabitants of the earth and those who take the mark of the beast will curse God for the judgments that will afflict them during the apocalypse.

Obviously a **lawless and evil world** will not welcome God's intervention and this is why we read in Revelation how the inhabitants of the earth blame and curse God for their judgments; a clear sign of unrepentant spirits and rebellion against the most high. We can read in the following passage just how corrupted man's soul will become as they curse God:

Rev. 16:8-9 - *"Then the fourth angel poured out his bowl on the sun, and power was given to him to scorch men with fire. And men were scorched with great heat, and **they blasphemed the name of God** who has power over these plagues; and they did not repent and give Him glory."* (**also read Is. 13:10-11; Joel 2:31**)

During the millennium, after Satan is locked away, the Lord will rule the entire earth and the remnant will all the inhabitants of the world will realize that there is and always was only ONE God!

Zechariah 14:9 *"And the Lord shall be King over all the earth.*
In that day it shall be "The Lord is one" and His name one."

God uses the Nations and Mankind to execute His Judgments

As He has always done throughout the age of man, God uses man to execute His plans and will. God gave man dominion over the earth and this is why He rarely directly interferes in the affairs of man. Notwithstanding, God remains in control of all things, even during the apocalypse. God also uses mankind and the nations to **fulfill His word**. The following passages reveal this.

Rev. 17:17 - *"For God has put it into their hearts **to fulfill His purpose**, to be of one mind, and to give their kingdom to the beast, **until the words of God are fulfilled**."*

Jer. 1:19 - *"They will fight against you, but they shall not prevail against you. For I am with you," says the Lord, "to deliver you."*

Note: God will allow many nations to invade Israel at the time of the end, but they will not prevail **(Is. 5:28; Joel 2:4; Joel 2:5).**
The following passage could be referring to ISIS which sprang up from the East, and like he east wind gathering and beheading captives. It could also be another sinister group that forms an end time Caliphate; or other nations that unite to attempt to destroy Israel and God's elect. Time will tell, but make no mistake about it, God remains in control and no one fully knows when and how the end time scenario will play out and who the final players will be.

Habakkuk 1:9-11 - *"They all come for violence; their faces are set like the **east wind**. They **gather captives** like sand. They scoff at kings, and princes are scorned by them. They deride every stronghold, for they heap up earthen mounds and seize it. Then his mind changes, and he transgresses; he commits offense, ascribing this power to his god."*

Below is another clear **indication that terrorist factions may indeed be instrumental forces that may help** trigger the apocalypse.

Is. 33:18-19 - *"Your heart will **meditate on terror**: "Where is the scribe?*
*Where is he who weighs? Where is he who **counts the towers**?" You will not see a fierce people, a people of obscure speech, beyond perception, of a stammering tongue that you cannot understand.*

The mark of the beast and a global economy/government is now a potential reality. With the advanced technology of computers, the Internet, and microchips, you can assign a number to every human being and gather data on just about anybody and their whereabouts. This will allow an end time global government to be able to track and locate anyone unwilling to accept a mark on their hand or Forehead - thus making the "Mark of the beast" prophesied in **Revelation 13:16-17** below a modern day possibility and reality.

Revelation 13:16-17 - *"He causes all, both small and great, rich and poor, free and slave, to receive a mark on their right hand or on their foreheads, 17 and that no one may buy or sell except one who has the mark or[a] the name of the beast, or the number of his name."*

In a later chapter, we will see the reasons why God will soon Judge the world.

Proof # 84 - False Peace

Every nation seeks peace, and many will align themselves with the coming one world government to secure peace. But the prophecies are clear that just as there has never been lasting peace throughout this age that it will be impossible to have peace at the time of the end; in a world full of iniquity and void of the Holy Spirit and God's veil of protection. The prophecies in this section should make that point very clear.

The Antichrist will use this desire for world peace to deceive many into thinking that he and his beast kingdom can exact some measure of peace at the time of the end. Of course he will back out of the peace agreement at the middle of the seven year pact (**Daniel 9:27**) as this false peace agreement will just be a ploy to allow him to grab global power.

Fallen man looks to fellow man and their elected leaders for peace, but history makes it clear that peace without God is impossible. Jesus is the only way to lasting peace; this is why He is referred to as the Prince of Peace. Yet at the time of the end the antichrist who will be hailed as a messiah, will mimic Christ and will offer a 7 years peace treaty which of course will not stand.

Daniel 11:21 - *"And in his place shall arise a vile person, to whom they will not give the honor of royalty; but **he shall come in peaceably**, and seize the kingdom by intrigue."*

Note: The antichrist will come upon the scene as a peaceful man, and will take over the world through his deceptive cunning, just like Satan deceived Adam and Eve at the Garden. He will come up with a clever plan for world peace, which as the following verse reveals, he will break his peace covenant in the middle of the agreement (a seven year peace agreement).

Daniel 9:27 - *"Then he shall confirm a covenant with many for one week;* **But in the middle of the week He shall bring an end to sacrifice and offering***. And on the wing of abominations shall be one who makes desolate, even until the consummation, which is determined, is poured out on the desolate."*
1 Thessalonians 5:3 - *"For when they say, "Peace and safety!" then sudden destruction comes upon them, as labor pains upon a pregnant woman. And they shall not escape."* (read also **Is. 13:6-9)**

Note: This verse is an end time prophecy which reveals that there will be a false treaty and false sense of security that will somehow allow the antichrist to gain the trust of the nations and enable him to establish a global government (**Rev. 13**)

Isaiah 48:18 - *"Oh, that you had heeded My commandments! Then your peace would have been like a river, and your righteousness like the waves of the sea."*

Isaiah 48:22 *"There is no peace," says the Lord, "for the wicked."*

Jeremiah 9:8 - *"Their tongue is an arrow shot out; it speaks deceit; one speaks peaceably to his neighbor with his mouth, but in his heart he lies in wait."*

Note: This prophecy has already been fulfilled with all the false peace agreements between Israel and its neighbors to date. These false peace accords have only allowed Israel's neighbors to fortify their strongholds, and to increase instability and violence in the Middle East region and throughout.

Revelation 6:1-2 - "*Now I saw when the Lamb opened one of the seals;[a] and I heard one of the four living creatures saying with a voice like thunder, "Come and see." And I looked, and behold, a* **white horse**. *He who sat on it had a bow; and a crown was given to him, and he went out conquering and to conquer.*"

Note: Soon the **horsemen of the apocalypse** will emerge on the scene with the first one riding a white horse and having a bow but no arrows - giving the impression of peace. But he will open the door to riders on Red, black and ashen horses symbolizing war, famine and mass death (**Rev. 6:3-8**)

Zephaniah 3:17, 3:5, 15 - There will be peace in Israel and the world, only when the Lord returns after the apocalypse. The reason for this is that lasting peace is alien to a world ruled by the prince of darkness. Once the Prince of Peace returns, only then can we have any lasting peace.

The Quest for Control of Jerusalem may trigger the Great Tribulation (Apocalypse/World War III)

Despite numerous attempts throughout this age to destroy the descendants of Israel, she remains in control of Jerusalem. Today Israel seems to be hated by all of its neighbors, and in fulfillment of **Zechariah 12:2-3**, Israel remains a heavy stone against her enemies as none of her adversaries have been able to remove her from her land; this despite numerous attempts since she was re-birthed in 1948.

Zechariah 12:2-3 - *"Behold, I will make Jerusalem a cup of drunkenness to all the surrounding peoples, when they lay siege against Judah and Jerusalem. And it shall happen in that day that I will make Jerusalem a very heavy stone for all peoples; all who would heave it away will surely be cut in pieces, though all nations of the earth are gathered against it."*

Israel has been and continues to be threatened by its neighbors, who lay claim to Jerusalem and all of the land of Israel the land that God promised to Abraham, Isaac and Jacob. God would later change Jacob's name to Israel to identify his descendants- the Jews as the nation of Israel.

Ez. 36:1-5 - *"And you, son of man, prophesy to the mountains of Israel, and say, 'O mountains of Israel, hear the word of the Lord! 2 Thus says the Lord God:* **"Because the enemy has said of you, 'Aha! The ancient heights have become our possession**, *therefore prophesy, and say, 'Thus says the Lord God:* **"Because they made you desolate and swallowed you up on every side, so that you became the possession of the rest of the nations, and you are taken up by the lips of talkers and slandered by the people**" *therefore, O mountains of Israel, hear the word of the Lord God! Thus says the Lord God to the mountains, the hills, the rivers, the valleys, the desolate wastes, and the cities that have been forsaken, which became plunder and mockery to the rest of the nations all around; therefore thus says the Lord God: "Surely I have spoken in My burning* *jealousy against the rest of the nations and against all Edom,* **who gave My land to themselves as a possession,** *with wholehearted joy and spiteful minds, in order to plunder its open country."*

Ez. 36:7 "Therefore thus says the Lord God: "I have raised My hand in an oath that surely the nations that *are* around you shall bear their own shame."

Prophecies that reveal that Israel will be invaded in the last days of this age:

Ever wondered why Israel is such a powder keg ready to explode. Well it is one that eventually will erupt in what the prophecies reveal to be the final war called Armageddon. The following verses indicate that world war three will center on Israel and the surrounding region.

Zechariah 14:2-4 - *"For I will gather all the nations to battle against Jerusalem; the city shall be taken, the houses rifled, and the women ravished.*
Half of the city shall go into captivity, but the remnant of the people shall not be cut off from the city.

Then the Lord will go forth and fight against those nations, as He fights in the day of battle. And in that day His feet will stand on the Mount of Olives, which faces Jerusalem on the east. And the Mount of Olives shall be split in two, from east to west, making a very large valley; half of the mountain shall move toward the north
and half of it toward the south."

Note: This passage is full of end of day prophecies; the time of the very end. This is a neat summary of how most prophecy scholars believe the end of this age concludes. There will be the battle of Armageddon and or Ezekiel 38, where most of the nations of the world under the spell of the antichrist, Satan and his demons will invade Israel. Israel will once again be victorious, by the hand of God Himself. Messiah will return with His feet touching the Mount of Olives. He will enter victoriously through the East Gate of Jerusalem.

Simultaneously there will be a massive earthquake that will reduce all nations into rubble, as described in **Revelation 16:16-21**.

It was prophesied thousands of years ago that Jerusalem would become a **"burdensome stone"** to all the nations. Today, not a day passes by that we do not hear of turmoil in the Middle East and threats and conflicts surrounding Jerusalem. It seems like the three major religions, and all of Israel's neighbors want control of the Holy city at any cost.

Zechariah 12:2-3 *"Behold, I will make Jerusalem a cup of drunkenness to all the surrounding peoples, when they lay siege against Judah and Jerusalem. 3 And it shall happen in that day that I will make Jerusalem a very heavy stone for all peoples; all who would heave it away will surely be cut in pieces, though all nations of the earth are gathered against it."*

In the book of Ezekiel we read a more detailed description of the nations that will come against Israel in the battle of Armageddon. Some prophecy scholars believe that this may be a separate war that they refer to as the **Gog/Magog** war. In either case this will be an end time battle.

Ezekiel 38:1-6 - *"Now the word of the Lord came to me, saying, "Son of man, set your face **against Gog, of the land of Magog, the prince of Rosh, Meshech, and Tubal,** and prophesy against him, and say, 'Thus says the Lord God: Behold, I am against you, O Gog, the prince of Rosh, Meshech, and Tubal. I will turn you around, put hooks into your jaws, and lead you out, with all your army, horses, and horsemen, all splendidly clothed, a great company with bucklers and shields, all of them handling swords. **Persia, Ethiopia, and Libya** are with them, all of them with shield and helmet; **Gomer and all its troops**; the house of Togarmah from the far north and all its troops—many people are with you."*

Going into any more detail as to who these nations are is beyond the scope of this book. If interested in learning more on the end time battle(s) you may want to grab a copy of: **"Apocalypse Countdown 2015 to 2021"** by Robert Rite

God Himself will defend His land Israel in these last days

The following verse makes it clear to all Christians, Jews and everyone who believes in the God who has fulfilled all His promises and prophecies that Israel is God's land. The Israelites are merely the appointed custodians of His land.
At the time of the end the Lord will be zealous for His land, and will have pity on Israel. (**Joel 2:18**).

God will destroy the armies of the king of the North

that come to invade Israel at the time of the end
(**Joel 2:20**)

"For behold, in those days and at that time, when I
restore the fortunes of Judah and Jerusalem, I will
gather all the nations and bring them to the Valley of
Jehoshaphat ["the Lord judges"]. Then I will enter into
judgment with them there on behalf of My people and
My inheritance, Israel, whom they have scattered
among the nations; and they have divided up My
land" (**Joel 3:1-2**).
In the following passages we read how it is God
Himself who will destroy the invading armies at the
battle of Armageddon.

Ez. 38:21-23 - *"I will call for **a sword against Gog
throughout all My mountains**," says the Lord God.
"Every man's sword will be against his brother. And I
will bring him to judgment with pestilence and
bloodshed; **I will rain down on him, on his troops,
and on the many peoples who are with him,
flooding rain, great hailstones, fire, and
brimstone.** Thus **I will magnify Myself and
sanctify Myself, and I will be known in the eyes
of many nations. Then they shall know that
I am the Lord**."*

Is. 66:16 - *"For by fire and by His sword the Lord will
judge all flesh; and the slain of the Lord shall be
many."*

Ez. 39:6 - *"And I will send fire on Magog and on
those who live in security in the coastlands. Then they
shall know that I am the Lord."*
Below is a description of how God will destroy the
nations which invade His land at the time of the end,

at the battle of Armageddon, just before the return of the Messiah.

Zechariah 14:12 - *"And this shall be the plague with which the Lord will strike all the people who fought against Jerusalem: their flesh shall dissolve while they stand on their feet, their eyes shall dissolve in their sockets, and their tongues shall dissolve in their mouths."*

The slaughter will be so great that for seven months Israel will be burying the enemy corpses (**Ez. 39:7-12).**

It will be a great feast day for the birds of prey **(Ez. 39:17).**
God makes it clear that the nations surrounding Israel that have provoked her throughout this age shall bear their own shame - and this promise is by His own oath!

Ez. 36:7 - *"Therefore thus says the Lord God: "I have raised My hand in an oath that surely the nations that are around you shall bear their own shame."*
The Hereafter

Proof # 85

The God of the bible is the only God that can and has described how this age will end and also can offer a detailed description of what the hereafter will be like; even describing our future dwelling place in paradise - with the measurements thereof.

Although our loving parents may want to reveal our future destiny they simply are not equipped to do this.

But our God who is most abundant in grace, does reveal to us a portion of our future inheritance as children of the most high. Although I have no doubt that even much more than the following awaits His faithful in paradise, the following are some of our inheritance that the Lord reveals to His children elect:

1) God will establish His sanctuary in our midst - a new heaven and a new earth:

Revelation 21:1-4 *"Now I saw **a new heaven and a new earth, for the first heaven and the first earth had passed away**. Also there was no more sea. Then I, John, saw the holy city, New Jerusalem, coming down out of heaven from God, prepared as a bride adorned for her husband. And I heard a loud voice from heaven saying, "Behold, the tabernacle of God is with men, and He will dwell with them, and they shall be His people. God Himself will be with them and be their God. And God will wipe away every tear from their eyes; there shall be no more death, nor sorrow, nor crying. There shall be no more pain, for the former things have passed away."*

Ezekiel 37:26 - Moreover I will make a covenant of peace with them, and it shall be an everlasting covenant with them; I will establish them and multiply them, and **I will set My sanctuary in their midst forevermore**.

2) God's Kingdom will replace all nations on earth. In the first passage below, the stone is a symbol of Jesus (the Stone that the builders rejected in Luke 20L17) topples the image (symbolic of all the kingdoms on earth) and became a great mountain (Jesus Kingdom replaces all kingdoms). Let's read:

Daniel 2:35 - *"Then the iron, the clay, the bronze, the silver, and the gold were crushed together, and became like chaff from the summer threshing floors; the wind carried them away so that no trace of them was found. And **the stone that struck the image became a great mountain and filled the whole earth**."*

Dan. 2:44 - *"And in the days of these kings the God of heaven will set up a kingdom which shall never be destroyed; and the kingdom shall not be left to other people; it shall break in pieces and consume all these kingdoms, and it shall stand forever."*

1 Cor. 15:24 *"Then comes the end, when He delivers the kingdom to God the Father, when He puts an end to all rule and all authority and power."*

Obadiah 1:21 - *"*...and the kingdom shall be the **Lord's**. (**Rev. 11:15**)

Psalm 82:8 - *"Arise, O God, judge the earth; for You shall inherit all nations."*

3) When the Lord returns He will reign from Jerusalem.

This is why Jerusalem is such a powder keg. You see, a world ruled by the prince of darkness does not really want the Lord to return (whether they realize it or not). Fallen man is possessed by the pleasures of this world.

Zechariah 2:10-13 - *"Sing and rejoice, O daughter of Zion! For behold, I am coming and I will dwell in your midst," says the Lord. "Many nations shall be joined to the Lord in that day, and they shall become My people. And I will dwell in your midst. Then you* *will know that the Lord of hosts has sent Me to you. And the Lord will take possession of Judah as His inheritance in the Holy Land, and will again* **choose Jerusalem**. *Be silent, all flesh, before the Lord, for He is aroused from His holy habitation!"* **(Is. 12:6, 2:2, 3; Hab. 2:20; Deut. 32:9)**

The following passages also confirm that the Lord will establish His kingdom on the earth, and will eliminate or take over all the existing nations on earth.

Rev. 11:15 *"Then the seventh angel sounded: And there were loud voices in heaven, saying, "The kingdoms of this world have become the kingdoms of our Lord and of His Christ, and He shall reign forever and ever!"*

Rev. 21:1 - *"Now I saw a new heaven and a new earth, for the first heaven and the first earth had passed away. Also there was no more sea."*

Note: There will be no more sea because the nations will no longer be divided; all is under the control of the Lord!

Also, when the Lord returns, the nations shall beat their swords into plowshares, and their spears into pruning hooks. In other words, war will become extinct and there will finally be lasting peace **(Micah 4:3).**

4) The nations will flock to the New Jerusalem. Jerusalem will become as the earthly Throne of the Lord.

Is 60:8 - *"Who are these who fly like a cloud, and like doves to their roosts?"*

Jer. 3:17 - *"At that time Jerusalem shall be called The Throne of the Lord, and all the nations shall be gathered to it, to the name of the Lord, to Jerusalem. No more shall they follow the dictates of their evil hearts."*

What Heaven on Earth will be Like:

God even wanted to give us a good idea about our future home. The following passages describe the New Jerusalem which will be established when the Lord returns.

Rev. chapters 21 & 22 - provides an amazing and detailed description of the new heavens and earth. Let's review just a portion of these chapters:

"Now the wall of the city had twelve foundations, and on them were the names of the twelve apostles of the Lamb. And he who talked with me had a gold reed to measure the city, its gates, and its wall. The city is laid out as a square; its length is as great as its breadth. And he measured the city with the reed: twelve thousand furlongs. Its length, breadth, and height are equal. Then he measured its wall: one hundred and forty-four cubits, according to the measure of a man, that is, of an angel. The construction of its wall was of jasper; and the city was pure gold, like clear glass. The foundations of the wall of the city were adorned with all kinds of precious

stones: the first foundation was jasper, the second sapphire, the third chalcedony, the fourth emerald, the fifth sardonyx, the sixth sardius, the seventh chrysolite, the eighth beryl, the ninth topaz, the tenth chrysoprase, the eleventh jacinth, and the twelfth amethyst. The twelve gates were twelve pearls: each individual gate was of one pearl. And the street of the city was pure gold, like transparent glass." **Rev. 21:14-21**

We are even given the dimensions of the coming kingdom (the New Jerusalem)!

Ezekiel 48:16 - "These shall be its measurements: the north side four thousand five hundred cubits, the south side four thousand five hundred, the east side four thousand five hundred, and the west side four thousand five hundred."

Ez.40-48 - these eight chapters also describes the new city and temple.

For more insight on the Lord's kingdom on earth during the millennium you can read the following verses: **Zech. 6:15; Zech. 14:16-21; Is. 66:22-24; Zeph. 3:17, 3:5, 15**

Chapter 8 - The Miracle of the Human Body

Proof # 86

The human body is a miracle of creation in and of itself! It contains more than 1 trillion cells.   Just the retina in our eyes can conduct 10 billion calculations every second!

Just one simple human cell is much more complex than the most powerful computers. Carl Sagan once said that there exists the equivalence of 100 million Encyclopedia pages of information in just one human cell - all perfectly organized!

The Universe inside each of us

In this section I just want to share how our bodies are more complex, complete and even more significant to God than the entire cosmos.

God created man in His image, and through man the sciences, physics, and everything else - including the many atheists and nonbelievers who reject God's omnipotence and sovereignty by questioning His capabilities and authority. They thus relegate and credit the marvels of God's creation to some man-made theories such as **"big bang"** and **"evolution"**.

When you contemplate the miracle of the human body which contains an innumerable number of cells and billions of organisms within, it is not just a marvel, but it is as if the sovereign God of the universe created a mini-universe inside all of us. A microcosm (little world) that is so elaborate, that science will never fully master it - and **MOST DEFINITELY** will _**NEVER**_ be able to replicate it.

Indeed, there is a whole universe inside of us. And like the universe, it is all from God and as a result it all belongs to God. The word microcosm here implies that man is a condensed version of the whole universe!

The point I want to make here is that when you behold the miracle of our body, you behold the awesome glory of our creator. The glory of God is not only displayed in the universe and on earth, but inside each of us. God has put his spirit inside each of us. It is that spirit that lets us breathe and think, live and blink. Without God we are nothing but the dust that we came from.
We are composed of a mortal body and an eternal soul. Your choices while in this temporary mortal body will determine where your soul will reside in perpetuity".

We may indeed be the hieroglyphic of the universe - and since we are created in His image, God's DNA resides in all of us - either in a **pure form** or in a **corrupted form**! Our bodies were originally created with the perfect DNA of God, until original sin allowed Satan to corrupt our DNA and thus bring forth all kinds of sickness, suffering and iniquity.

So because of this corrupted DNA many allow Satan to plant evil thoughts in their mind, such as that we can be like god. We are not gods while in this mortal body; and even in the afterlife although some of us will be children of the most high, we will NOT be God.

This is what Lucifer wanted to be, and we can witness the mess that he has made of this current age.

The serpent wants us to think that we can persist living in sin thinking that there will never be a day of reckoning. The clay (dust) that we are can never be greater than the creator. It is for our sinful nature that we all must return to the ground.

Genesis 3:19 - *"In the sweat of your face you shall eat bread till you return to the ground, For out of it you were taken; **For dust you are, and to dust you shall return.**"*

God created man twice. What I mean here is that God clearly separated the physical man in us and the spiritual man in us. The spiritual man was created first, and then the physical man was created from the dust of the ground. The spiritual is eternal (representative of heaven) and the physical is mortal (representative of earth). The spiritual man is Holy while the physical man is representative of our sinful nature.

God also gave us two minds:

1) The spiritual, sanctified, redeemed holy Spirit filled mind

2) The physical, carnal, sinful, and corrupted mind

So God created the spiritual man on day six in His very own image: **Genesis 1:26** Then God said, "Let Us make man in Our image, according to Our likeness;…". So our spirit existed before our physical body!

In **Genesis 2:7** we then see that God created physical man. He formed man from the dust of the ground and then he breathed into his nostrils the breath of life (God's spirit in us). Out of the dust of the ground man became a living soul. So in us are a physical body and a spiritual eternal soul. So a portion of God's DNA is in all of us - as we are all destined to become children of God, **if we so choose**. Can you see how we are such a privileged and unique creation in the universe!

From the above remember the following: Since God created man on the sixth day - the number six is the number of man. God rested on the seventh day - and made it **Holy**, therefore the number seven is the number of God. Remember this number - we will explore it in the next section.

The Reincarnation Myth

Many have been sold into believing another one of Satan's half truths which is the myth of **reincarnation.** This is a demonic distortion of the strong possibility that our spirit man may have existed in heaven before we were placed on earth! Let's read:

Ephesians 1:4-5 " *just as He chose us in Him* **before the foundation of the world**, *that we should be holy and without blame before Him in love, having predestined us to adoption as sons by Jesus Christ to Himself, according to the good pleasure of His will,".*

Read also **Romans 8:2**; **Ephesians 2:4-10**.

Now let's explore some numbers and how they seem to connect the human body with Christ's number.

Unlike the English alphabet, the Greek and Hebrew alphabet were assigned numbers, and these numbers are given relevance. This is why in Revelation the **number 666** is assigned to the antichrist.

With that, let's see what the number for "**Lord Jesus Christ**" is. It totals **3,168**. The interesting part is that we find the root number of 3168 all over creation! Here are just a few examples:

- The air we breathe in encoded with "Lord Jesus Christ". Breathable air is 60 miles from ground to sky. That comes out to **316,800** feet; the root of which is **3168**. <u>Acts: 17:25b</u> reveals" "He gives to all life, breath, and all things".

- Our bodies consist of 60,000 miles of blood vessels. This is 316,800,000 feet, which again is the root of 3168: "**Lord Jesus Christ**"!

- The brain of an adult weighs **3.168** pounds!

Chapter 9 - Numbers Declare the Glory of God

Proof # 87

Does The Number Seven Provide Proof that the God of the Bible is the Sovereign God of the Universe?

God made it easy for mankind to believe that He is the sovereign God of the universe. Even numbers declare the glory of God! Many Bible scholars believe, as I do, that the number seven is the divine number of God. As we have covered, God created the heavens and the earth in seven days.

The significance of Numbers in the Bible

Just like it is the foundation of all science and mathematics; numbers are also very significant in the bible. Of all the numbers, the number seven and multiples thereof is a very significant number. Seven is the number of completion.

Seven is also the number that demonstrates how God is in charge of ALL things.

Here are just a few examples:

- There are 7 days in the creation sequence.

- God rested on the seventh day and made it Holy.

- There are 7 stars on Jesus right hand in **Revelation 1:20**

- the 7 lamp stands which are the 7 churches
Revelation 1:20

- Jesus addresses these seven churches of Asia (and I believe this is a message to all the churches throughout this age) in **Rev. 2-3**

- the 7 spirits of God in **Revelation 3:1**

- the 7 oceans on earth

- The 7 major continents on earth

- God also established a 7th year Shemita whereby the land was required to rest on the seventh year.

- From Exodus to the time Solomon dedicated the first Jewish Temple was 490 years or **70 x 7.**

- We see this very number at play again - from the dedication of the first Jewish temple (Solomon's temple) to the command of King Artaxerxes of Persia, which allowed the Jews to return to their land to rebuild the temple and Jerusalem, we have **490 years (70 x 7).**

- Then from the edict that allowed the Jews to return to their land and rebuild Jerusalem, to the Messiah Jesus Christ we again have **490 years (70 x 7).** Do you see a trend here? Do you think this is coincidence?

- Preceding the millennium, there will be a seven year tribulation period (the Apocalypse), whereby the earth will be refined with fire before the return of Messiah.

Note: For more revelations on the coming apocalypse read:
"Revelation Mysteries Decoded" by Robert Rite

- The tribulation will consist of **7** *seal judgments,* **7** *trumpet judgments* **and 7** *bowl (Vial) judgments.*

- Mankind has been allotted **6 days of one thousand years each** (**2 Peter 3:8**), and then there will be the seventh day of 1,000 years when the Messiah will rule the world during the millennium. During the 7th day - the 1000 year millennium, **mankind will rest** from Satan and sin; **a one thousand year Sabbath**, if you will!

- The number seven is in the laws of God such as the seventh day Sabbath. Also, God established a year of jubilee (**Leviticus 25:8-12**), to take place every **49 years 7 x 7**, as a year to let the land rest and restore itself. Yes the earth is a living organism but it is not to be worshipped as some "green earth movement" folks do.

- Our life revolves around a very structured seven day week, and God made it this way since the creation of man (**Genesis 2:2**) and this age. I believe He did this so that we really cannot escape the significance of the number seven. God designed it this way, so that the wise person is reminded of this sign every week of their life! Of course fallen man has changed the seventh day to fit other religious dogma - but God's calendar is firm!

I believe the number seven stands for eternity and it is our destiny for those who choose to be Holy children of God through perpetuity!

As you can see, God's total plan for mankind revolves around the number seven.
Other Numbers of significance in the Bible:

The Number twelve is quite significant also, it is the number of government:
- the 12 apostles
- the 12 tribes of Israel
- the 12 major constellations
- the 12 signs of the zodiac
- 12 pearly gates
- the 12 foundations in heaven
- 12 months in a year.

The number 3 is the number of divinity. For example:
- The Trinity consists of Father, Son, and Holy Ghost
- Jesus was resurrected from the dead on the 3rd day.

The number 6 is the number of man.
- Interestingly, man's body is composed of six main parts: a head, a torso, 2 arms and 2 legs.
- Also mans allotted time on earth is 6,000 years,
- Man is to work just 6 days (and rest on the seventh)
- and the Antichrist who will come out of the nations (a human being) is assigned the number 666.
The reason that I bring this up is because numbers also play a role in confirming certain signs. For example we see that the Zodiac consists of Twelve constellations, and each constellation has 3 Decans - that is right all twelve have exactly 3 Decans each. Then of course the fact that man was given 6,000

years on earth indicates that the signs in the heavens, and the coming Blood Moons may be pointing that the time of the end of this age may indeed be just around the corner.

Chapter 10 - The Heavens Declare the Glory of God

Proof # 88

The Constellations and other Signs in the Heavens Prove the Existence and Omnipotence of God

*"**The heavens declare the glory of God** and the firmament shows His handiwork. Day unto day utters speech and night unto night shows knowledge"* (**Ps. 19: 1-2**)

The Heavenly Bodies Cry out that there is a Creator!

Astronomy is the science of studying the movements of the stars and planets and that is acceptable to God. God Himself calls the stars all by name (**Psalm 147:4**), and tells us that the heavens were created for the telling of time and seasons, as well as for signs (**Genesis 1:14**).

Notwithstanding, these heavenly bodies are not to be worshipped as the astrologers, idol worshippers, and other occult practitioners do. God warned mankind of this very thing in **Deuteronomy 4:19:**

"And take heed, lest you lift your eyes to heaven, and when you see the sun, the moon, and the stars, all the host of heaven, you feel driven to worship them and serve them, which the Lord your God has given to all the peoples under the whole heaven as a heritage."

That said, since the dawn of this age man has been fascinated by the magnificent beauty of the heavens. There are many signs for us to discern in God's great billboard in the sky (the universe).

It appears that the truth of God was encoded in the heavens long before the written word, as a testimony of the sovereignty, omnipotence and the glory of God Almighty. God's bible was written in the night sky long before the dawn of this age!

There are twelve major zodiac signs (constellations) in the heavens and amazingly these 12 zodiac signs are recognized by every nation and kingdom since the dawn of this age. It is believed by some that these zodiac signs predate any other writings. The Persians and Arabians credit the identification of these signs to Adam and his sons Seth and Enoch.

The twelve Zodiac signs have existed from the beginning when God said "**let them be for signs**". All religions, ancient artifacts, hieroglyphics, and civilizations since before the written word, have the exact same twelve signs, in the exact same order, and with the same image. It's as if they were planted in the heavens with a manual that labeled each one of them for us
The Zodiac is a ring of twelve star groups called constellations that are organized in such a manner as to form images or pictures.

Each one was ascribed a name and was given a divine picture or story behind them. Following are the names of each of these constellations: Virgo, Libra, Scorpio, Sagittarius, Capricorn, Aquarius, Pisces, Aries, Taurus, Gemini, Cancer, Leo.

Long before Abraham or Moses walked the earth, and before Homer wrote his Odyssey and Iliad, we find evidence of the divine significance of the zodiac signs in the oldest book in the bible which is actually the book of Job. After persevering great trials, God intervenes. But first He enlightens Job with many divine truths. In **Job 38:31-33** God declares the following:

"Can you bind the cluster of the Pleiades, or loose the belt of Orion? Can you bring out Mazzaroth in its season? Or can you guide the Great Bear with its cubs? Do you know the ordinances of the heavens? Can you set their dominion over the earth?" **Job 38:31-33**

NOTE: In the above passage, God is making reference to "**Mazzaroth**".
Mazzaroth is a Hebrew term for: "the Constellations of the Zodiac"! God here is confirming the antiquity and authenticity of the zodiac as scriptural signs! Mankind influenced by Satan, has distorted the truth behind all of the signs in order to align them with the myths, false gods, goddesses and other idols of the ancient Greeks, Babylonian and other early civilizations.

He also makes reference to the constellations:

In the book of Job we find references to some of the constellations including:
- Cetus, the sea monster (referred to as Leviathan)
- Draco, the great dragon

Below are biblical references to the Zodiac/Constellations:

Virgo - Revelation 12:1-2,5
Draco the Dragon - Revelation 12:3
Venus (Isa. 14: 12);
Saturn (Amos 5: 26);
the Pleiades (Job 9: 9; 38: 31; Amos 5: 8);
Orion (Job 38: 31; Amos 5: 8);
Arcturus (Job 9: 9; 38: 32) ;
the twelve signs of the Zodiac (Job 38: 32-33;
Isa. 13: 10; Judges 5: 20).
Isaiah 27: 1; Isaiah 13:10; Job 41: 1; Job 26: 13;
Ps. 104: 25-26; Psalm 9:1-4; Job 38:31-33

As if that is not enough proof, in **Job chapters 38 and 39**, we are given the twelve Signs of the Zodiac!
Battles of heaven - Job 38: 37
Lions - Job 38:39
Ravens - Job 39:41
Wild goats - Job 39:1
Hinds - Job 39:1
Wild ass - Job 39: 5
Unicorn 39:9
Peacocks -Job 39:13
Ostrich - Job 39:13
Horse - Job 39:19
Hawk - Job 39:26
Eagle - Job 39:27

Proof # 89 - Clearly, the signs of the Zodiac have a divine meaning

The prophet Amos also makes specific reference to the constellation Orion in the following verse:

"Seek Him that makes the seven stars and Orion" (Amos 5: 8).

Indeed, God created the star groups called the Zodiac. The bible refers to these signs in the night sky as the **MAZZAROTH**. These signs reveal a wonderful picture of creation and redemption. They display pictures of the ongoing battles between the prince of this world, and the God of heaven - between the serpent (Draco) and the Lion of the tribe of Judah (Leo). The zodiac as well as all prophecy points to Jesus Christ as the King of the Universe! These affirm the revelation of the word contained in the bible. As Revelation declares: "...For the testimony of Jesus is the spirit of prophecy" **Revelation 19:10**.

As indicated earlier, the bible declares in **Jeremiah 33:22** that the host (stars) of heaven cannot be numbered. Only in the last 100 years have astronomers confirmed what the bible revealed thousands of years ago, that the number of stars in the universe cannot be counted by man; some estimate however that perhaps one sextillion (that is a 1 followed by 21 zeros) stars exist in the universe - an uncountable number indeed! Yet our awesome creator has named every single star!

 Psalm 147:4 *"He counts the number of the stars; He calls them all by name."*

Jeremiah 33:22 *"As the host of heaven cannot be numbered, nor the sand of the sea measured, so will I multiply the descendants of David My servant and the Levites who minister to Me."*

Each Zodiac sign is a picture of one or more of the following:

1) the Messiah
2) the trials of each believer
3) the schemes of the serpent - Satan
4) the progressive battle between good and evil
5) the church - the body of Christ

The constellations (zodiac) display the history of mankind and the ongoing cosmic battle between good and evil. The bible teaches that God Himself has named all the stars:

Psalm 147:4 "He determines **the number** of **the stars** and **calls them each by name**."

The signs of the heavens are signs from God. God reveals this in **Genesis 1:14**: ***"And God said, "Let there be lights in the firmament of the heavens to divide the day from the night, and let them be for signs and seasons, and for days and years."***

The word ***"Signs"*** here most definitely implies that the heavens may have foretold before the dawn of this age the outcome of that galactic battle between good and evil. The prophecies have been unveiled for us from the beginning of time.

Your destiny has nothing to do with the month you were born, but rather everything to do with whom you choose to place your trust and faith upon. **Your month of birth is insignificant since, as you shall see, every single zodiac sign reveals that God controls all 12 months; He is in control of everything.**

For example, four of the zodiac signs clearly reveal the fate of the serpent (Satan).

During Jesus 3 1/2 year ministry he was the suffering Messiah. In the first half of the tribulation period (3 1/2 years) just before His return, through the zodiac **"Leo the Lion"** we witness in heaven that Jesus is bestowed the crown and title of *"the **Lion of the Tribe of Judah**"* **Revelation 5:5, after He defeats the serpent (Draco the Dragon).**

The constellations (**zodiac**) are indeed God's word displayed in the heavens. They are most definitely the signs for the age of man.

Proof # 90 - Now let's explore some additional details on what we have already covered and some other heavenly signs outside of the constellations:

1) The Constellation Leo (symbolic of Jesus) contains the star **Regulus**. It is the brightest star in the constellation and one of the brightest stars in the night sky. It is appropriately referred to as the "***King star***".

2) *"Crown of Thorns Galaxy"* This galaxy was discovered in 2009 by the Hubble telescope that looks just like the crown that was placed on Jesus head prior to His crucifixion. In the center of this galaxy is a very bright star or object. I believe that this is symbolic of Christ, who is the light of the world - and this light is positioned right in the middle of the crown of thorns! (Google it and see it for yourself!)

3) In 1973 there were 7 eclipses (Sun and Moon together). The Yom Kippur war occurred that year. The Arab oil Embargo started that year, 28 nations suffered one of worst doubts in history, and scientists observed one of the largest solar explosions in the Sun.

4) In **Rev 12:1-3** we read of a great wonder in heaven; a woman (symbolic of Israel) and a red dragon (Satan). Satan has been at war with the nation of Israel from the moment it was founded. Did you know that this supernatural battle has been grafted in the heavens? When we study the constellations, **we see Draco the dragon** (symbolic of Satan) with his eyes fixated upon **Virgo** (symbolic of the Virgin with bearing the Messiah child), **as if it poised to attack and devour her**!

5) A major prophetic event took place in 1967. On that year Jerusalem was reunited with Israel during the infamous six day war. **From 1967 forward, astronomers have observed an increase in cosmic activity,** including but not limited to increased sunspot activity, the lunar landing in 1969 and the shoemaker levy comet strikes.

6) In Genesis 37:9-10 - Joseph (a symbol of Jesus) had a dream where the sun, moon and stars bowed before him. This dream revealed that Jacob and his 11 sons would someday bow down to Joseph as the 2nd in command under Pharaoh in Egypt. This dream actually reveals how the Jews will bow before their Messiah at the time of the end, when he returns for the second time; this time as the King of Kings of the world.

7) The fallen angels and their Nephilim seed (Genesis 6:1-3), taught astrology, worship of stars, and mythology. They corrupted God's word pictures in the heavens. They made Gods of the constellations, sun, moon and stars. From this evil seed grew the mythology that the Egyptians, Greeks, Romans, Babylonians and most other empires throughout this age embraced as part of their culture. These became the gods that they would worship.

8) In the Jewish calendar time is circular (Ecclesiastes 1:9). The astronomical calendar (constellations) begins with Virgo (Virgin bearing a child - symbolic of the Messiah's birth **Luke 1:27),** and ends with Leo the Lion (Jesus the Lion of the Tribe of Judah **Rev. 5:5)**.

9) **The Constellation Cetus** in Greek mythology refers to a sea monster. The tail of this constellation covers 1/3rd of the stars of heaven (called the Southern Cross). Revelation 12:4 reveals how Lucifer, now Satan, caused one third of angels **(referred to as stars in Rev. 12:4**) to be cast out of heaven! Mere coincidence? Not!

10) **Cetus** in Greek mythology is a land and sea **monster**. It has a horn between the eyes and a star behind its neck. **Cetus** is referred to as the rebel, and also as the destroyer (just like Satan is referred to). **Revelation 13:1** reveals that another type of **monster** - the Antichrist (referred here as a beast) comes out of the sea and **Rev. 13:11** reveals that the false prophet comes out of the Earth. *The Antichrist also has a little horn (Daniel 7:8), just like Cetus*!

11) **Revelation 1:20** refers to the mystery of 7 stars and lamp stands. This is referring to the seven churches. This also has a related cosmic sign. Church is a Greek feminine word meaning "Eklesia". There are 7 stars in the heavens which form a part of Pleiades M45; a 7 star formation on the neck of Taurus the bull. Speaking of Taurus, Jesus is holding the 7 stars in his right hand in Revelation representing the 7 churches. These 7 churches in revelation were located in Turkey at the base of the "**TAURUS**" Mountains in Asia Minor - *what a coincidence*!

12) In **Rev 12:1-3** we read of a great wonder in heaven; a woman (symbolic of Israel) and a red dragon (Satan). Satan has been at war with the nation of Israel from the moment it was founded. Did you know that this supernatural battle has been grafted in the heavens? When we study the constellations, *we see Draco the dragon* (symbolic of Satan) with his eyes fixated upon *Virgo* (symbolic of the Virgin with the Messiah child), *as if it poised to attack and devour her*!

13) **The Hale-Bopp Comet** - was first discovered in 1995 because it very rarely passes the earth. It's much brighter than Haley's comet. On 7/23/1995 it was spotted inside Sagittarius (half beast/half man).

In 1998 it exited out of Orion during the Feast of Pentecost. The war on terror started 4 years later. When a comet passes Orion it is believed to be a sign of the end of an age.

Astronomers have determined that prior to the mid 1990's Hale-Bopp was last seen 4200 years ago when Noah was building the ark! "As it was in the days of Noah, so it will be at the coming of the Son of Man." **Mathew 24:37**

14) - To Hebrew scholars **1998 is a significant year**. It is the Hebrew year 5758. The 5 and 8 add up to the name of Noah. They believe it indicates that 1998 began the seasons of Noah. ***"As it was in the days of Noah, so it will be at the coming of the Son of Man."*** Mathew 24:37

15) ***"Hand of God Nebula"*** discovered by the Hubble space telescope; it looks like a massive hand with fire shooting out of its fingers! Could this be a sign of the coming tribulation whereby the sequence of judgments includes fire coming down from heaven?

16) The Star of Bethlehem: During the birth of Jesus there was significant activity in the heavens; both literally and physically. God may have created a temporary new star called the star of Bethlehem. Perhaps the star was a conjunction of Jupiter and Saturn which history has signified major event. It could also have been a comet. Such a comet was observed in 5 BC in China. There was also a conjunction (joining of several stars) in 2 BC. All of these incidents were happening during the time of Jesus birth. These alignments were for signs.

Upon Jesus death there was also a strange sign from heaven: *"From noon until three in the afternoon darkness came over all the land."* Mathew 27:45

Proof # 91 - The Shemita

God established a Shemita every seventh year which would be a Sabbath year for the Lord. On this seventh year the land was required to rest and the fields would be opened to allow the poor and the beasts of the field to feed. Blessings or curses would flow depending on whether the nation kept or violated the statutes during this 7 year period.

Prophecy scholars such as Jonathan Cahn have noted that since 2001 the seven year Shemitah cycles have triggered curses instead of blessings. So far in this young century we have had two Shemita years.

- **2001** - 9/11 terrorist attacks. In 2001 Wall Street's market lost **7%**

- **2008** - Financial markets meltdown. In the 2008 crash **7%** - when the final bell rang to close the stock market the key index was down **777 points**!

- The phenomenon is intensifying and now we have **2015**! The next shemita is scheduled for 2015 and many signs converge in 2015 indicating that the beginning of ominous times may be imminent.

The following passage could be referring to the blood moons and other signs that will be converging in the 2014 to 2016 timeframe:

Joel 2:30-31, 3:15 - *"And I will show wonders in the heavens and in the earth: Blood and fire and pillars of smoke. The sun shall be turned into darkness, and the moon into blood, before the coming of the great and awesome day of the Lord."*

For more information on these and many other signs, you may want to consider grabbing a copy of the following new releases both by Robert Rite:

"Blood Moons Rising"
"Signs in the Heavens"
"Apocalypse Countdown 2015 to 2021"

Chapter 11 - Global Warming or God's Warning?

Proof # 92

Thousands of years before man coined the term "global warming" the ancient prophets foretold that in the last days we would experience an increase in weather disturbances such as rising water levels (**Jeremiah 47:2**). In the past few years America has had weather issues that have been so extreme that there is no way it could be defined as normal. Strange would be a better term.

Proof # 93 - Strange Weather

There are many examples of freak weather phenomena throughout the USA and the world. below are just a few examples:

The year 2010 was a grab bag of worldwide natural disasters. That year was the deadliest in more than a generation. Earthquakes, heat waves, floods, volcanoes, super typhoons, blizzards, landslides, and droughts killed more than 260,000 people.

In the United States erratic weather patterns have become the norm. One day it seems warm and sunny, and the next day it's cold and rainy. In the northeast it seems to rain every day. For example, spring 2013 and 2015 were so cold it seemed like an extension of winter! Many in the northeast complain that spring seems to last a few weeks instead of three months. For example, In 2012, the northeast and other parts of the USA experienced the warmest spring on record. A year later in 2013, they had one of the coldest spring seasons on record.

Record Flooding

In 2011, there was record flooding in the Mississippi and Missouri area (USA). In 2012 a massive drought managed to create record-low levels at the very same rivers which a year earlier had been overflowing their banks. In 2013, the cycle has reverted back to flooding at the Mississippi river and surrounding area.

Record Tornado Outbreaks

In 2011, America also experienced the worst Tornado outbreak in the nation's history. We didn't just set one or two records we established a whole series of new milestones for tornado activity. After all the deadly weather in 2011, the next year was the quietest year on record for the Midwest. Some states set records for not seeing a single tornado!

The tornado that hit the town of Moore, Oklahoma

(USA) in 2013 with winds upwards of 200 mph was one of the most destructive tornadoes that America has ever seen. It actually stayed on the ground for a record 20 minutes. That tornado came almost two years to the day after the deadliest tornado in U.S. history hit Joplin, Missouri.

Sinkholes

Over the past few years, giant sinkholes have appeared at an unprecedented rate, in California, Pennsylvania, Florida, and other areas of the USA and the world. In Harrisburg, PA alone - at least 41 sinkholes have been reported!

In 2013, a 37 year old man named Jeffrey Bush from Tampa, Florida died when the earth underneath his home suddenly opened and swallowed him up - his body was never found. His entire bedroom was swallowed deep into the earth.

In one housing division in the Spivey's neighborhood in Lake County
(about 100 miles north of San Francisco), a 600-square-foot garage disappeared from a home - dropping 10 feet below the street. Soon the homes on both sides collapsed as the ground gave way

Proof # 94 - Intensifying Earthquakes (Matthew 24:7)

The bible prophesied that in the last days there will be an exponential increase in earthquake intensity and frequency (**Matt. 24:7**). From 2004 to 2014 there has been an alarming increase in earthquakes registering 8 or higher in the Richter scale. 18 quakes of Mw8.0 or greater were recorded since December 2004; a rate of more than twice that from 1900 to 2004.

Earthquakes are becoming more frequent and more powerful. The "**Ring of Fire**" continues to heat up. Over the past few years, there have been major earthquakes in almost every area. The only area remaining is the west coast of the United States. The US geological service recently reported that from 2008 to 2010 the earth has experienced 107,135 earthquakes. America alone experienced 25,449 of these earthquakes, or slightly less than a quarter. Hmmm is God sending a message to "the greatest nation on earth". Are we paying attention yet? The book of Revelation prophesizes that the last of the 7 great plagues will be a massive worldwide earthquake that may even topple mountains. (**Rev. 16:17-20**)

Wildfires

We have experienced 6 of the 10 worst years for wildfires ever recorded in the United States since 2000.

Drought

The western U.S. is currently experiencing the worst stretch of drought since the days of the Great Depression.

Volcanic Activity

We also see escalating volcanic activity. Most recently, a major volcanic eruption occurred in 2014 in Alaska forcing disruptions in air travel, among other effects. It has sent up ash as high as 22,000 feet.

Record Snow Storms

Then there is record snow. Cities and States such as Rapid City, S.D., Duluth, Minn., Boulder, Colorado, Boston, and New York have all endured their snowiest years recorded. In some areas weather records go back more than 100 years! Recently, there were more than 1,100 snowfall records and 3,400 cold weather records set across the nation. In 2013, for the first time ever, Arkansas received snow in the month of May!

Hurricanes

Once upon a time, hurricanes in the north east were considered unlikely - perhaps a 200-year event. In 2012 Hurricane Sandy caused wide-scale destruction as it slammed into the East Coast of the U.S. The NYC Subway System was flooded in the worst disruption in its 108 years of operation. Long gas lines erupted as deliveries to refineries stalled. A record high water level of 13.88 feet was set in Battery Park (lower Manhattan), breaking the oldest official record of

10.02 feet. Sandy's central pressure bottomed out at 940 millibars, setting a record for the lowest pressure of an Atlantic storm north of Cape Hatteras, NC. Sandy was the largest land-falling Atlantic tropical cyclone, which had tropical storm force winds extending out to 600 miles. Tropical Storm Irene was also a bad storm, but it was a baby compared to hurricane Sandy.

Indeed, the frequency and gravity of escalating disasters is alarming! March, 2011 when Japan suffered its worst recorded earthquake in its history - seems like a distant memory. So does January, 2010 when 250,000 people were killed by another quake that struck Haiti. Yet just a century ago the world could go a decade or more without witnessing or experiencing one of these major calamities.

So what does all of this have to do with proof that the bible is the inspired word of God?

I believe that Bible prophecy is the only way to account for the oddities of Mother Nature lately. ***God warned that the calling card of the Tribulation hour would be an increase in weather anomalies.*** The on-and-off pattern may be God trying to get Man's attention. However, since that doesn't seem to be working, I look for the warning signs to be replaced with judgment.

"And there shall be signs in the sun, and in the moon, and in the stars; and upon the earth distress of nations, with perplexity; the sea and the waves roaring; men's hearts failing them for fear, and for looking after those things which are coming on the earth." Luke 21:25-26

I firmly believe the "birth pains" prophecies are the reason we are seeing so many events with "**100 year**" label. We've said it before, but it deserves to be said again. **Nothing is as true as the fact that God is this world's chief weather maker. The book of Job unequivocally states this fact:** *"God thunders marvelously with His voice; He does great things which we cannot comprehend. He says to the snow, 'fall on the earth'; likewise to the gentle rain and the heavy rain of His strength." Job 37:5-6*

In **Luke 21:11** Jesus warned us all that in the last days the world would experience exactly what we are experiencing today.

"And there will be great earthquakes in various places, and famines and pestilences; and there will be fearful sights and great signs from heaven."

Luke 21:11

There has been some effort by the media and entities with a political agenda, to blame all this strange weather on what was once called global warming but now operates under a more ***"politically correct" term - climate change***. Environmentalists did well when they were arguing that greenhouse gasses were causing the earth to warm up. But then they ran into trouble when the mercury started to plunge. Even if there is some unknown component that can account for a drop in the temperature, the change can't account for the rapid change in weather.

Peter spoke very passionately of these last days concerning the kingdom of God on earth, "...And I will show wonders in heaven above, and signs in the earth beneath; blood, and fire, and vapor of smoke: The sun shall be turned into darkness, and the moon into blood, before that great and notable day of the Lord comes: And it shall come to pass, that whosoever shall call on the name of the Lord shall be saved." **(Acts 2:17-21)**

The Bible has promised that this coming judgment will be so overwhelming to the unprepared multitudes that, "**Men's hearts failing them for fear, and for looking after those things which are coming on the earth: for the powers of heaven shall be shaken." (Luke 21:26)** Our present moon is the heavenly body that determines the tides of the oceans.

When the moon starts to convulse the earthly water tables will follow suit. The Son of God told us this would occur. **"And there shall be signs in the sun, and in the moon, and in the stars; and upon the earth distress of nations, with perplexity; the sea and the waves roaring." (Luke 21:25)** The

East and West coasts of America may experience tidal waves that could devastate entire major cities.

Man thinks that having an "Earth Day" or two can circumvent or stop God's coming Judgments! Wrong.

In the end, there is no safe place in this world. Between earthquakes and hurricanes, fires and tornadoes, evil decisions made by us and our leaders in government. We're all in constant danger. ***Our only hope in these last days is the Lord!***

There is only one "pollution" that matters to God, *and it is not the pollution of earth's atmosphere - it is the pollution of man's soul!*

"The earth is polluted because its inhabitants, because they have transgressed the laws, violated the

statutes, and broken the everlasting covenant. Therefore the curse has devoured the earth, and those who dwell in it are desolate.

Therefore the inhabitants of the earth are burned, and few men are left." **Isaiah 24:5-6**

Chapter 12 - The Big Bang Theory Declares the Glory of God

Proof # 95

Whether there indeed was a big bang or not, the key question is:
"who created the Big bang; the Bang or the Creator"?

I do not believe in the Big Bang theory, however the creator may have created the universe with a "big bang" if He so chose to. But it does not make sense since the creation account reveals that the earth and the universe were created in an orderly fashion, not a random process. The big bang theory seems to be the only theory that those who do not want to credit a creator can come up with!

Note that the first words God declares is "Let there be light", and a big bang would certainly create light and energy. But a "big bang" did not create life, God did; along with the big bang itself - if there was one.

The problem with modern science is that it wants to credit nature for everything so that they can deny the existence of a creator - as if their admittance that there indeed exists a creator would leave most scientists without a job. The root of the problem I believe is that from the beginning man has always wanted to play God - to take credit for discovering the truth; when the truth has been staring them right in the face from time immemorial.
All the discoveries that man has made are by the grace of God - the creator of the universe. If man would have heeded the ordinances, statutes and

wisdom contained within the scriptures no doubt man would have harvested an even greater multitude of blessings and an even greater quality of life then we enjoy today.

Many scientists admit that there are many universal laws that do not support a theory that an orderly Universe can evolve from a chaotic explosion. Order cannot come out of disorder - such as the big bang. Even Stephen Hawking, a leading expert on the cosmos admits that the big bang theory does not answer how man and the rest of the Universe came from in the first place.

The "Big Bang Theory" doesn't answer the most important question - what or who caused the explosion. Matter and energy have to come from somewhere. Kent R. Rieske reasons: "We know that matter can be created out of energy, and energy can be created out of matter. This doesn't resolve the dilemma because we must also know where the original energy came from."

Here are some other reasons why the Big Bang theory does not make sense:

- Explosions do not create - they destroy. So to postulate that the big bang created the universe makes no sense at all.
- Explosions do not cause order - they cause disorder.
- The theory does not address where all the matter in the universe came from.
- The theory cannot answer where the energy come from that caused this explosion?
- The scientific law called "**conservation of angular momentum**" would require that if there was a big

bang then all the planetary objects, including the planets and their moons would all spin in the same direction - and this is not the case.

- The Big Bang theory violates the First law of Thermodynamics, which states:
"matter cannot be created or destroyed"

- The theory also violates the "Second Law of Thermodynamics" which states that "everything tends towards disorder" over time.

- Since the big bang could only have created chaos and not an orderly universe, then why does science conclude that it is the most logical theory?

The bible teaches that everything waxes old (wears away) like an old garment (Psalm 102:25-27; Hebrews 1:10-12).   This coincides with the second law of thermodynamics which states that the universe is wearing down rather than "evolving".

The Big Bang singularity may be nothing more than a Big lie that Satan has managed to delude the mind(s) of scientists who I believe would rather believe in something absurd and ridiculous rather than admit to a divine creator.

Chapter 13 - Darwin's Dilemma and Much More

Proof # 96

The "Rigid" mindset of most scientists restricts their ability to understand and accept the supernatural realm where our creator operates.

According to most geologists, the Earth is 4.7 billion years old. If we take the creation timeframe in Genesis literally, then God surely did create the universe in almost an instance (days rather than billions of years). After all God is God, and nothing is impossible for him. What humans and scientists consider improbable can occur instantly in the supernatural realm, given the awesome power of God.

Our mere mortal minds cannot fathom the power and the glory of almighty God. Man's limited capacity to understand the supernatural and infinite capacity of the creator limits the ability for the scientific mind to accept the truth as revealed in God's word! This is not only Darwin's dilemma but the dilemma of all non-believers as well.

In this section we will explore some of the holes in the theory of evolution. Let's begin.

The Evolution Delusion

Our DNA is unique and no other living organism or animal has our DNA. This is why humans can only produce humans and monkeys cannot produce men! God made this perfectly clear in **Genesis 1** where He emphasized how all of God's creation will always reproduce after their own kind.

In the creation account, it is revealed that everything that God created was for Good and remains good. It was pure and perfect - infused with the DNA of God! Everything that mankind has since created, can be used for either good or evil because it is imperfect. It cannot be perfect for it is inherently made imperfect by the corrupted DNA of the prince of this world. When we ate from the tree of the knowledge of good and evil - we mixed good with evil and became corrupted; imperfect. From then on our minds would always doubt and strive to replace the creator and His ordinances with ours.

Our God is the God of science. Sadly, many people and scientists are trying so hard to discredit God as the true creator of this glorious universe and all the goodness thereof that they have fabricated "theories" on just about anything that could possibly persuade the masses into losing all faith in the creator. Science cannot prove the theory of evolution, nor that we are linked in any way to primates.

The reason for this is that the Theory of Evolution is not a scientific law or a law of biology. A scientific law must be 100% correct. Failure to meet only one challenge proves the law is wrong. This section proves that the Theory of Evolution fails many challenges.

According to the bible and bible prophecy we were created in God's and only God's own image (**Genesis 1:26**). We were not created in the image of an ape or monkey. God created man from the dust of the ground and breathed life through man's nostrils.

Man did not evolve from Apes - he evolved from God

Evolutionists have lined up pictures of similar-looking species to claim that they evolved over a long period of time. The human "family tree" is a prime example. Petrified skulls and bones from species of extinct monkeys and apes are lined up in an effort to present a gradual progression from monkey to modern man. The missing link is not an ape-man - it is monkey species that became extinct. There are many species that have become extinct throughout this age.

Even "Lucy" which evolutionists sold as proof of man evolving from apes was another deception. She was merely a young female ape; with a head, arms shoulders and legs like an ape - because she was an ape!

Apes and humans are genetically quite different. As **DarwinConspiracy. com** explains: "the human Y chromosome has twice as many genes as the chimpanzee Y chromosome and the chromosome structures are not at all similar."

Man has not been around for one million years

Evolutionists want us to believe that man has been around for 1 million years or so. Common sense would disprove this. Let's consider two key points:

1) First, many scientists agree that carbon dating and radioisotope dating is far from an exact science.

2) More importantly, if man were around for a million years or so as evolutionists suggest, then the population of man would not be just 7 billion - it would have to be in exponentially greater - perhaps in the trillions!

3) The population of man in the 7 billion range coincides with biblical records dating man approximately 7000 years on earth!

4) If man is 1,000,000 years old, why did air travel, computers, cell phones and almost all high tech innovations materialize in just the past century?

The earth is not millions of years old

Bible dating and prophecy tells us that the earth is not millions of years old. Since 1829 the **strength of the earth's magnetic field** has decreased by approximately 7%. If the field gets too weak then life on earth would not be possible! It is believed that the half life of the magnetic field is 1,400 years, which proves that the earth is not millions of years old; the magnetic field would have been already too weak to sustain human life hundreds of thousands of years ago!

Given the above calculations, Dr. Thomas Barnes, former Emeritus Professor of Physics at the University of Texas in El Paso, calculated that given the strength of the magnetic field, life on earth would have been impossible more than 20,000 years ago - which is much more supportive of bible dates, rather than carbon dating.

The absence of transitional Fossils:

There is an absence of transitional fossils which is a serious dilemma for evolutionists! Even some of the most famous evolutionists in the world acknowledge the complete absence of transitional fossils in the fossil record.

For example, Dr. Colin Patterson, former senior paleontologist of the British Museum of Natural History and author of "Evolution" once wrote the following...

"...I fully agree with your comments about the lack of direct illustration of evolutionary transitions in my book. If I knew of any, I would certainly have included them...there is not one such fossil for which one could make a watertight argument."

Below are some additional points that discredit evolution and that support the biblical account:

- Even the smallest single-cell organism has millions of atoms forming millions of molecules that must each be arranged in an exact pattern to provide the required functions. The cell is self sufficient with an energy-producing system, protective outer skin, control system, reproductive system, and its own operating system like a mini brain! This requires an intelligent creator - it is impossible for **such an incredible marvel to have happened by chance**.

- Fossils cannot exist unless there was a major flood that buried and quickly solidified.

- The earth's Strata confirms that animals did not evolve - they were **suddenly created** at specific timeframe. If the theory of evolution was true, we should not see a sudden explosion of fully formed complex life in the fossil record. Yet that is precisely what we find.

The sudden appearance of complex life in the fossil record is so undeniable that even **Richard Dawkins** has recognized this dilemma..."It is as though they [fossils] were just planted there, without any evolutionary history. Needless to say this appearance of sudden planting has delighted creationists. Both schools of thought (Punctuationists and Gradualists) despise so-called scientific creationists equally, and both agree that the major gaps are real, that they are true imperfections in the fossil record. The only alternative explanation of the sudden appearance of so many complex animal types in the Cambrian era is divine creation and both reject this alternative."

- Anything that we dig up that is supposedly more than **250,000 years old** should have absolutely **no radiocarbon in it whatsoever**. **Radiocarbon** is supposed to disappear in a few thousand years. But instead, we find it in everything that we dig up – even dinosaur bones, and other relics that are supposedly millions of years old. This is clear evidence that the "**millions of years**" theory may be just that - a theory.

For instance, CMI has over the years commissioned and funded the radiocarbon testing of a number of wood samples from 'old' relics such as Jurassic fossils, Triassic sandstone, etc. These were published by Dr Andrew Snelling in Creation magazine and the Journal of Creation. In each case, the dating results were in the thousands of years, instead of millions of years.

After many studies (including studies from the RATE group) the findings confirm that virtually all biological specimens, no matter how old they are supposed to be, show measurable C-14 levels. This effectively limits the age of **all buried** fossils, relics and organic specimens to less than 250,000 years old.

- The Grand Canyon did not take billions of years to form. It would have been able to form from a global flood in accordance with the biblical account of Noah's flood.

- In the 1980 Mount Saint Helen volcanic eruption, trillions of pounds of sediment were pulverized. Yet today we see new formations throughout that area as if nothing ever happened - all in the span of just 30 years!

- There are fossilized sea shells near top of Mt. Everest - which support the biblical account of a great flood. There are accounts from all over the world and throughout civilizations about a great worldwide flood.

- The Theory of Evolution claims that organic life was created from inorganic matter. That is impossible. The top scientists in the world having limitless lab resources and instruments remain unable to transform inorganic matter into a single organic living cell.

A new species has never been developed by science. In fact, the most modern laboratories are unable to produce the simplest of proteins as found in humans and animals.

- No species has ever been proven to have evolved in any way. New species cannot evolve by natural selection. Modern scientific theory and discoveries are proving evolution to be impossible.

- The odds make it **astronomically impossible** for even a simple single cell organism to simple evolve, given that it contains more than 60,000 proteins in 100 different configurations all perfectly organized.

- If natural selection were true, Eskimos for example would have grown body fur to adapt to the cold climate, but they don't.

- Contrary to the theory of evolution - fossil layers are not found in an evolutionary order. The fossil layers are actually found out of order contrary to the textbooks on evolution.

Evolutionists believe that the ancestors of **birds developed hollow bones over thousands of generations** so that they would eventually be light enough to fly. This sounds wonderful if one does not believe in God or believes that God created birds with heavy bones - and then realizing His error He fixed it - and even then it took him thousands of years to fix His mistake. This does not even make sense or logic within the theory of evolution itself.

- The fossil record itself disproves the evolution theory.
What we observe are new species that seem to explode onto the scene out of nowhere. New fossil discoveries continue to disprove evolution to be wrong.

- In "Evolution: A Theory in Crisis by **Michael Denton**"; Michael Denton says, "Despite the tremendous increase in geological activity in every corner of the globe and despite the discovery of many strange and hitherto unknown forms, the infinitude of connecting links has still not been discovered and the fossil record is about as discontinuous as it was when Darwin was writing the Origin."

H. Matthews, British biologist and evolutionist, recently concluded: "The fact of evolution is the backbone of biology, and biology is thus in the peculiar position of being a science founded on an unproved theory." Even the originator of evolution had to admit that it is not provable, and more and more scientists are coming to the conclusion that it is a lost cause.

R. Danson reported in the New Scientist: "The theory of evolution is no longer with us, because neo-Darwinism is now acknowledged as being unable to explain anything more than trivial change, and in default of some other theory, we have none."

Stephen Jay Gould, Professor of Geology and Paleontology at Harvard University, once wrote the following about the **lack of transitional forms**..."The absence of fossil evidence for intermediary stages between major transitions in organic design, indeed our inability, even in our imagination, to construct functional intermediates in many cases, has been a persistent and nagging problem for the gradualist accounts of evolution."

Stephen M. Stanley of Johns Hopkins University has also commented on the **stunning lack** of **transitional forms** in the fossil record..."In fact, the fossil record does not convincingly document a single transition from one species to another."

Time Magazine made the following statement about the lack of evidence for the theory of evolution..."Yet despite more than a century of digging, the fossil record remains maddeningly sparse. With so few clues, even a single bone that doesn't fit into the picture can upset everything. Virtually every major discovery has put deep cracks in the conventional wisdom and forced scientists to concoct new theories, amid furious debate."

<u>The universe is winding down; slowing down to a lower state, not higher</u>. Yet evolutionists want us to believe that organisms are evolving into a **"better"** species over time - as if what God created was inferior; even though God declared that it was good enough:

<u>Genesis 1: 31</u> "Then God saw everything that He had made, and indeed it was very good."

The genes of plants, insects, animals, and humans are continually becoming defective, not improving. Species are becoming extinct, not evolving. Order will always move naturally towards disorder or chaos. We observe this same phenomenon when we watch the evening and world news and observe how society is also degrading with rampant iniquity throughout the globe. Our "modern" society does not offer a better quality of life than our ancestors enjoyed. Sure we have better toys and gadgets - but how is the quality of our air, or crime rate to mention just two?

Malcolm Muggeridge, the world famous journalist and philosopher, once made the following statement about the absurdity of the theory of evolution…"I myself am convinced that the theory of evolution, especially the extent to which it's been applied, will be one of the great jokes in the history books of the future. Posterity will marvel that so very flimsy and dubious a hypothesis could be accepted with the incredible credulity that it has."

What a shame that what he expected did not come to pass, because evolution is still a widely held belief, even among some Christians! The evolution deception is right out of Satan's handbook of delusion - a very intoxicating mix indeed for the unguarded mind!

Proof # 97 - The Miracle of the Earth

The miracle of the earth itself dispels the theory of evolution in that the odds of everything that allows this planet to sustain life to have happened by chance and disorder are astronomically incalculable.

- If the earth were just 10% larger or smaller - life would not exist.

- The earth is perfectly situated from the sun; if it were just a bit closer it would be too hot on earth to sustain life, a bit further and it would be too cold for life.

- If the average temperature on earth were just 2 or 3 degrees higher the north and South poles would melt and major cities would be approximately 200 feet underwater!

- The materials the stars and the sun are made of are not the materials that would materialize from an explosion. For example the sun contains no dust.
- If the magnetic forces within our planet were any stronger or weaker - our planet could not sustain life.

- The earth's tilt on its axis is perfect as it allows the sun to cover the entire planet and allow for more vegetation and habitation; as well as for the changing of the seasons.

- The earth's revolution every 24 hours makes it possible for life - otherwise one half of the planet would be frozen and in total darkness and the other would be an uninhabitable scorched desert.

- The moon produces the tide which replenishes the oceans with oxygen that allow the fish to breath.

Proof # 98 - The Human DNA Declares the Glory of God
The Miracle of our DNA

The odds of even a single sell "assembling itself" by chance is astronomically incalculable. The following is an excerpt from **Jonathan Gray's** book entitled "**The Forbidden Secret**" "...Even the simplest cell you can conceive of would require no less than 100,000 DNA base pairs and a minimum of about 10,000 amino acids, to form the essential protein chain. Not to mention the other things that would also be necessary for the first cell."

 "To put it another way, if you attempted a trillion, trillion, trillion combinations every second for 15 billion years, the odds you would achieve all the correct orientations would still only be one chance in a trillion, trillion, trillion, trillion … and the trillions would continue 2755 times! "It would be like winning more than 4700 state lotteries in a row with a single ticket purchased for each. **In other words...it is impossible.**"

There is no scientific evidence that a species can change the number of chromosomes within the DNA. The chromosome count within each species is fixed. This is the reason a male from one species cannot mate successfully with a female of another species, and why man could not have evolved from a monkey. Each species is locked into its chromosome count and it cannot be altered without adverse effects.

Mutations destroy information (DNA). Mutations are DNA replication errors and are always regressive to its host. Mutations are very rare and when they occur they are unpredictable and destructive to the species. They can lead to diseases and defects. Mutations result in an inferior species - not a superior species. They never lead to a new or enhanced species - that is an evolutionary lie.

The DNA of an organism cannot change or mutate from external influences or environmental adaptation. Darwin apparently had no clue of this when he developed the theory. DNA only changes during the reproductive process as the organism absorbs chromosomes from the male and female donors.

DNA is so incredibly complex that it is absolutely absurd to suggest that such a language system could have "evolved" all by itself by accident...When it comes to storing massive amounts of information, nothing comes close to the efficiency of DNA. **Scientists believe that a single strand of DNA** is thousands of times thinner than a strand of human hair. One pinhead of DNA could hold enough information to fill a stack of books stretching from the earth to the moon 500 times.

Although DNA is wound into tight coils, your cells can quickly process the information stored in DNA. DNA even has a built-in accuracy checker that ensure precise copying, with a near perfect accuracy ratio of roughly one mistake every **10 billion nucleotides** that are copied.

DNA is a code, a language and not just a molecule with a pattern. It is super compact information storage mechanism. All codes are created by a conscious mind. There is no natural process known to science that creates coded information like DNA does. Don't let our fallen scientific minds deceive you. There exists absolutely no empirical examples of a code or language that occurs naturally. Don't believe another of Satan's lies, promulgated by "modern" science - it is all part of the original "theory" or should I say "lie" that Satan spewed at the Garden of Eden that we can be like God; this side of heaven!

Darwinists believe that the human brain developed without the assistance of a creator. What is most unbelievable is that there are intelligent beings out there that actually believe this! The human brain is a miracle in and of itself and as close to a supernatural organism as it gets. The following is how a PBS documentary described the complexity of the human brain: "**It contains over 100 billion**

cells, each with over 50,000 neuron connections to other brain cells."

The human cell has 46 chromosomes (23 pairs), and this does not change. This is why people will always give birth to people, and monkeys to monkeys. This coincides with God's creation account as we read below, and note how God wanted to emphasize how everything produces **"after its own kind"**:

Genesis 1:24-25 - *"Then God said, "Let the earth bring forth the living creature according to its kind: cattle and creeping thing and beast of the earth, each according to its kind"; and it was so. And God made the beast of the earth according to its kind, cattle according to its kind, and everything that creeps on the earth according to its kind.*
And God saw that it was good."

Our brain is an awesome organ yet mankind's ability to create is still far inferior to what God already created at the beginning of this age. Our abilities are limited to our brain capacity - which in itself is a miracle creation of God and as already proven - is impossible to have evolved from a big bang or through evolutionary process. But God's ability to create is beyond mortal man's capacity. Science believes that it can eventually be like God - this is just Satanic delusions, and to coin an appropriate phrase "delusions of grandeur". It is about time scientists humble themselves before the creator and admit that they cannot even replicate a single cell or a DNA strand - let alone improve on what God created before the dawn of man!

The whole theory of evolution seems to just be a demonic attempt to replace the creator with nature; by ascribing God's glory and omnipotence to a "mother nature" or other force that does not exist outside of the creator. The quest for mankind to try to play God, by trying to replicate God is futile and it will certainly fail. If anything it will only lead to inferior or defective mutations. Mankind has not even been able to create a snowflake that is superior to the original! Only God can. Folks, this is all just common sense! A copy of an original will never be the original, and will never look as good as the original. A masterpiece painting of Rembrandt is priceless, but a copy is cheap. It is because Rembrandt died and can no longer produce originals. God created all the masterpieces in 6 days, and so He rested on the 7th day. Everything that was good for this earth and its inhabitants, was already created by God! Everything created afterwards is a counterfeit and inferior.

There is no need for evolution since God is done with His original work on earth which God saw that it was good; but His **greatest masterpiece** awaits His faithful in Paradise!

Proof # 99 - The Miracle of Israel Declares the Glory of God
How Israel and the Jews Prove the existence of the God of the Bible

Israel's endurance and resilience despite its erratic history is a sign that God exists and remains in control despite all the evil forces and nations that hate the Jews today. Although 6,000,000 Jews died during the holocaust, they flourish today. So many nations have tried to annihilate Israel throughout this age, yet all have failed. Today, the city of Jerusalem persists under the Israeli flag.

The Hebrew language also survived all of the Jewish people's evictions from their land. **Zeph. 3:9** refers to the Hebrews as a people of pure language; a chosen language. The Torah scroll is written in Hebrew. If there will be a spoken language in heaven perhaps it will be in the Hebrew language.

The failed attempts to relocate Israel

When we consider the history of all nations, it is nothing short of a miracle that the Jews returned to their exact land despite having been disbursed twice. Before the nation of Israel was reborn in 1948, they were almost re-established in other places such as Alaska, French Madagascar, and Oblask (Russia). In 1903 for example, they were almost offered the nation of Uganda in Central Africa by the British. None of these plans materialized because it was not the will of God! It was the will of God that the Jews would be given back their homeland which would house God's Holiest ground - **Jerusalem**!

The failed attempts to change the name of the Jewish homeland

In 1948 they wanted to name Israel and Jerusalem differently; offering up names such as Judea, Palestine, Zion, etc. But this was NOT the will of God. so the land that the Jews were to re-occupy would be named what God wanted it to be named - so it was named **Israel**!

When the UN was briefed that the new homeland for the Jews would be called Israel they were outraged and many threatened to resign! General Marshall predicted that it would lead to war in the Middle-East. Later on Truman would equate himself to Cyrus who had allowed the Jews back to their homeland from ancient Persia.

Call the re-establishment of Israel and the Jews back to their original homeland a miracle or not; but it most definitely is the hand of God on all matters pertaining to Israel throughout this age!

Many political historians agree that Truman was most likely re-elected with the votes of the Jews because he supported and embraced the establishment of the Jewish homeland, despite the resistance of some in his cabinet and the US State Department who did not want a Jewish state.

It is strange that anyone of the US would resist a Jewish state, since Jews were instrumental in helping to end World War II. One such person was a genius by the name of Albert Einstein who was instrumental in inventing the nuclear weapons that helped end WW II. The use of just 2 of these atomic bombs on Japan helped save millions of American and Japanese lives had America invaded Japan! Since then, the fear of the use of Nuclear weapons has helped prevent millions of lives as it has deterred aggression from many nations including Russia. We can thank the Jews again for another invention, which in this case helped end the worst war in history!

Jerusalem - the Rejoicing Stone

After the 1967 war when the Israelites recaptured Jerusalem, a stone was discovered on the western side of the Wailing Wall. On it was etched the following verse from **Isaiah 66:14**

"when you see this your heart shall rejoice, and your bones will flourish like an herb". I believe this is a fulfilled prophecy that once Jerusalem is recaptured at the time of the end it will never change hands again until the Messiah's second coming!

This may have also fulfilled the following prophecies:

Habakkuk 2:11 - "for a stone shall cry out of the wall."

Nahum 2:5 - "they shall make haste to the wall and thy defense shall be prepared"

The prophet Jeremiah prophesied that the exodus from the Gentile nations would be greater than those out of the exodus from Egypt. Whereas **600,000 Hebrews** came out of Egypt during the exodus, after 1948 over **1.5 million** Jews returned from Russia, South Egypt, Ethiopia and other parts of the globe. *"Therefore behold, the days are coming," says the Lord, "that it shall no more be said, 'The Lord lives who brought up the children of Israel from the land of Egypt,' but, **'The Lord lives who brought up the children of Israel from the land of the north and from all the lands where He had driven them**.' For I will bring them back into their land which I gave to their fathers."*
Jer. 16:14-21

More Proof that the God of the Bible is in full control of all the kingdoms of the world!

Many kingdoms throughout this age have tried to wipe Israel out of the map...

- Assyria tried and failed - and they are no more.
- Egypt tried and their army became fish food in the Red Sea!
- Babylon tried - to this day the city lies in ruins.
- Rome tried to crush them and their Empire eventually collapsed.
- The Byzantines failed.
- Adolf Hitler tried and he ended up committing suicide while Germany lay in rubble.
- Russia tried to oppress them and that regime collapsed.
- Today as has been the case over the past few decades, the terrorists and Iran want to wipe Israel out. According to God's word, they too will fail.
At the battle of Armageddon the world's armies under the influence of Satan will make one last ditch attempt but this time God Himself will wipe them out.
The nation of Israel still stands and will stand until Messiah returns on the Mount of Olives - Jerusalem - this is God's promise; and while heaven and earth will pass away His word will never end.

So why does the world shun or ignore the meaning and significance of Israel?

First we have to come to grips by accepting that we are living in a *fallen* world that has no clue about the divine significance of Israel, Jerusalem and its people. And the inhabitants of the earth in these last days are very busy, and focused on themselves and their problems. Many do not care or do not want to care about the fate of little Israel, its significance and contributions to mankind, or any of God's truths for that matter, because they would rather pre-occupy themselves with their technology games and gadgets, social media and entertainment and the preoccupations of these last days - rather than to dedicate a little time for their creator. For many, or should I say most, the **matters of life** overshadow the only one that **really matters** this side of heaven.

Israel is now gas independent, and converting most of their vehicles to gas instead of oil so that they can be oil independent as well.
- They have their own farming; and such abundance that they can export much of it! Yet it is just the size of the state of New Jersey.
-Technology breakthroughs are occurring at such amazing rates that some believe Israel will eventually find a cure for every disease

Satan's hatred of Christians, Israel and the Jews confirms the Glory of God:

God's prophecies all revolve around Israel. This is probably the main reason that Satan hates Christians, Jews, Jesus, Jerusalem, the word and indeed the world! He hates everything that God created that was good. But there are also other reasons why he hates God's creation. Let's review a few:

1) Israel is the only nation whereby God entered into a covenant with and whereby god named its city after His name.

2) Israel is the only nation that built on earth a

replica of God's dwelling place in heaven. The **Ark of the Covenant** was built by Moses in the wilderness and granted God access to the earth! The tabernacle built under Moses was patterned after the heavenly temple - thus giving God access to the earth and its people every year on the Day of Atonement.

3) Israel received and gave to the world the word of God through His prophets.

4) Through the Hebrew bloodline the Messiah Jesus would come to the world offering redemption to the unsaved. Christ would be from the tribe of Judah. He would not only be called to be the savior of the Jews, but of the whole world. Satan is trying real hard and succeeding in this fallen world to conceal this truth from fallen man.

5) Because Satan knows that Israel's continual existence is divine proof for the wise, that there is a God that created and controls the destiny of mankind and the nations, and that He exists in heaven.

6) The coming of Christ is connected to the restoration of Israel and the return of the Jews. Interesting how it is estimated that 600,000 men came out of the Exodus from Egypt, and 607,000 returned immediately to Jerusalem in 1948 (although greater numbers would follow)! Mere Coincidence - I do not think so.

7) Because Satan knows that the restoration of Israel means that it is curtains down for him! He knows that Israel's restoration in 1948 as a nation started the end time clock, and the time of his end ticks nearer. The devil is well aware of the following prophecy:

Isaiah 2:2 - *"Now it shall come to pass in the latter days that the mountain of the Lord's house shall be* *established on the top of the mountains, and shall be exalted above the hills;* and all nations shall flow to it."

8) Because if he can capture and defend Jerusalem - then the Messiah cannot return. He actually thinks he can defeat God. But as we have already addresses God will use Israel as bait for Satan and his armies to invade Israel at the end of this age and the devil and his armies will become bird food at the **Valley of Megiddo (battle of Armageddon)**!

Why will God Judge the World?

I assume you already know the answer to this or at least have a good idea. But to make sure we are all clear on this, let me list some of the more significant reasons. In ***"Revelation Mysteries Decoded"*** I explained that the earth needs to be cleansed of iniquity before the Messiah can return. In this section let's review some of the reasons why cleansing is required.

1) The World is full of iniquity and lawlessness.

Due to rampant lawlessness, the Lord has already warned the world that He will return with fire to judge all flesh.

The Antichrist is referred to as "***the Lawless one***", so obviously there will be rampant lawlessness when he takes over during the tribulation period.
But please do not think for a moment that lawlessness

is relegated exclusively to the tribulation period. It already runs rampant in the U.S. and throughout most of the world. Any doubts just watch the evening news. If it does not make you sick, sad, disgusted or depressed then you have become somewhat desensitized to the lawless world that we live in today - and that is not necessarily a good thing! The hardening of the spirit or the heart is the work of Satan and the media and government play a huge part in this evil brainwashing of our collective minds.

So instead of immersing yourself into the filth that the media and entertainment industries spew out, you really need to set aside the **world** and immersing your mind and spirit in the **word**. The Lord set aside one day each week for us to clear our minds of the things of this world and feed and fortify our minds and souls with the things that make for peace. If you do this, I guarantee that this will make you feel much better.

America, along with most "modernized" nations in their self righteous arrogance, has made legal what God has forbidden from the very beginning. And yet mankind continues to ask: ***"Why would a loving God exact such great judgment upon our earth during the Apocalypse"***?

God most assuredly will judge, and He clearly explains the "why" to us in many places throughout the bible including the following passage:

Isaiah 24:5-6

*"The earth is polluted because of its inhabitants, **because they have transgressed the laws,***

violated the statutes, and broken the everlasting covenant. Therefore the curse has devoured the earth, and those who dwell in it are desolate. Therefore the inhabitants of the earth are burned, and few men are left."* (also read **Isaiah 66:15-16; Rev. 19:12; Rev. 19:15)**

2) Mankind's Rejection of the Lord: Just before the Lord's return **the inhabitants of the earth will have become such *devil worshippers*** that they even initiate a global feast day when God's two witnesses sent to the earth to evangelize the world are killed during the apocalypse in the streets of Jerusalem by the Antichrist (Revelation 11:10). During the time of the end, the false prophet of the Antichrist will be performing great miracles, and because of the lack of knowledge of the truth, many will believe he is the long awaited Messiah.

These lost souls have rejected God and the word, and prefer the kingdom of Satan on earth, because they "think" they can do and get away with whatever they please, and whatever pleases them! *I know this sounds like science fiction; sadly it is NOT!*

3) The Nations want to divide up God's Land.

From the very beginning, the nations of this fallen earth have been "Hell-bent" (pun intended) on *dividing up God's land* (Jerusalem & Israel) that God gave to a chosen people. I believe that a main reason for this is that Satan knows that the New heavens and new earth will be established in the area of Jerusalem, so he wants to take over that area so as to spoil God's plan. *He has deluded the minds of fallen man and the leaders of the nations so that they have cultivated this everlasting hatred for Israel and its people throughout this age*.

One of the reasons is that the nations are "***hell bent***" on dividing Israel and Jerusalem up for an illusory peace! This peace is an ungodly and unholy kind of "peace", because it violates God's land covenant with Israel, which threatens Israel's very existence, contrary to the will of God.

The word of God makes it clear that Jerusalem is the city of God, and that the land of Israel was promised to the Jews. Let's read some of many verses whereby God tries to make this absolutely clear!

Psalm 132:13; psalm 48:1-2,8; Psalm 137:5-6; Psalm 121:4; Zechariah 14:1-2; Isaiah 24:23; John 10: 10. Genesis 17:18-19; Isaiah 54:1; Genesis 21:10; Galatians 4:21-31; Genesis 12:1-7; Genesis 13:14-15; Genesis 15:7-10; 15:17-21; 22:16-17; Gen. 25:5-6; Gen. 26:1-6; Genesis 28:10-13; Exodus 3:8; Exodus 6:2-4; 6-8; Lev. 26:42; Numbers 34:2; Deuteronomy 1:8; Joshua 1:2-4; 1 Kings 8:36; 1 Chronicles 16:13-18; 2 Chronicles 6:25; Nehemiah 9:15; Psalm 105:8-11; Psalm 121:4; Isaiah 60:21

God declared thousands of years back that Israel would re-emerge as a nation. This was fulfilled in 1948. **Here are just a few prophetic references to this truth**: Jeremiah 30:3; Ezekiel 36:9-10; 24; 28; Amos 9:14-15; Zechariah 2:8

Throughout the bible, we see how God exacts Judgment upon those who try to divide Israel

up. We read of this in Joel 3:2, Nahum 1:2, Joshua 10:11 (God stoned to death the nations that tried to harm Israel during their 40 year journey in the wilderness), Haman (a Persian leader) and his family were hung to death when he tried to do the same to the sons of Israel. **Yet mankind still does not get it**?

What is incredible to ponder is that ***the world consists of 196,939,900 square miles and Jerusalem occupies only 49 square miles!*** Yet there is all of this rage, controversy, jealousy, and turmoil over such a tiny parcel of land. In fact, the fight for Jerusalem will lead mankind to the final global war, which will result in the death of billions of souls (yes, and all of this is prophesied in the bible), most will not even know why they went to war to begin with.

Joel 3:1-2 - *"For behold, in those days and at that time, when I bring back the captives of Judah and Jerusalem,* **I will also gather all nations, and bring them down to the Valley of Jehoshaphat; and I will enter into judgment with them there on account of My people, My heritage Israel, whom they have scattered among the nations; they have also divided up My land.***"* (**Jer. 30:3; Zech 14:2**)

*".....And it shall come to pass in that day, that **I will seek to destroy all the nations that come against Jerusalem***" **(Zech. 12:4-9).**
"All who rage against you will surely be ashamed and disgraced; those who oppose you will be as nothing and perish. Though you search for your enemies, you

will not find them. Those who wage war against you will be as nothing at all." **Isaiah 41:11-12**

The hatred of the Jews and their current control over Jerusalem is the center of the controversy that **Zechariah 12:2-3** and **Zechariah 14:1-3** speaks of reserved for the last days.

Psalm 83 warns all of those nations that continue to threaten Israel in an effort to **_"destroy them as a nation, that the name of Israel be remembered no more" (Psalm 83:4)_**.

Zephaniah 2:8-10 - "I have heard the reproach of Moab, and the insults of the people of Ammon, with **which they have reproached My people, and made arrogant threats against their borders.** Therefore, as I live," Says the Lord of hosts, the God of Israel, "Surely Moab shall be like Sodom, and the people of Ammon like Gomorrah; over-run with weeds and salt pits, and a perpetual desolation. The residue of My people shall plunder them, and the remnant of My people shall possess them."

This they shall have for their pride, **because they have reproached and made arrogant threats against the people of the Lord of hosts**." **Is. 16:6** Below we read how at the time of the end the Lord will exact vengeance upon all the nations surrounding Israel that have mocked, hated and attacked them from the days of old to present. **God will remember all of the arrogant threats of Israel's neighbors and He will judge them all at the time of the end (when they invade Israel at the battle of Armageddon).** Let's read:

Zechariah 14:12 - *"And this shall be the plague with which the Lord will strike all the people who fought against Jerusalem: their flesh shall dissolve while they stand on their feet, their eyes shall dissolve in their sockets, and their tongues shall dissolve in their mouths."*

Note: Zechariah 14:12 reads like the symptomatic effects of advanced nuclear weaponry; perhaps neutron bombs. But these may actually be the weapons of the Lords indignation as revealed in **Jer. 50:25**. Let's read:

Jeremiah 50:25 - *"The Lord has opened His armory, and has brought out the weapons of His indignation; For this is the work of the Lord God of hosts in the land of the Chaldeans."*

4) Because of the Persecution of His chosen people - the Jews.

Many ask, why would the God of the universe place such an emphasis on such a small plot of Land (Israel is about the size of the state of New Jersey) and the Jewish people; who are a race of merely 14,000,000 souls? It is ***because God had selected Israel and the Hebrews as a model for the world. Had the Jews followed God's model (which they didn't) then the world would not have turned out as corrupted as it is today. He also wanted to demonstrate to man, how with so little He could do so much! Through the bloodline of the Jews we were blessed with God's word, His statutes, the scriptures, the prophecies, The Messiah, and the way to eternal life with God as kings and***

144

priests in paradise forever (Rev. 5:9-10)! Let's read:

"You are worthy to take the scroll, and to open its seals; for You were slain, and have redeemed us to God by Your blood out of every tribe and tongue and people and nation, **and have made us kings and priests to our God**; *and* **we shall reign on the earth.**" **Revelation 5:9-10**
Yet from the first day that they became a unique race to God, the Jews have been a persecuted race.

Here are a few Examples:

- Pharaoh of Egypt
- King Nebuchadnezzar of Babylon (Iraq)
- Haman's plot (Persia/Iran)
- Epiphanies
- Titus
- Hadrian
- King Herod
- The Spanish Inquisition
- The Nazi Holocaust
- The Pogroms of Russia
- The 1967 and 1973 wars
- And others

The Nazi extermination camps where over six million innocent Jews and their families were sacrificed to the god of this world - Satan, is a testament of the everlasting hatred between the seed of Satan (all who worship and or do Satan's dirty work) and seed of God (His chosen people and the body of Christ). The Nazi's called these atrocities **"the Final Solution" to the Jewish problem**.

There is a day of reckoning coming called the "**the**

Great Day of God the Almighty" and "the Day of the Lord's Anger"; **which will be** *"GOD's FINAL SOLUTION" to the "fallen man" problem*!

In that day God will show the world and its inhabitants what He thinks of what mankind and their chosen leaders have done to His people and to His Holy land - **God is very patient (as He gives man sufficient time to repent) but He has NOT forgotten!**

5) Because they Broke God's Everlasting Covenant.

In the following passage, God reveals **3 more reasons** why the inhabitants of the earth are judged in the near future: because they have transgressed the laws, violated the statutes, and broken the everlasting covenant.

Is 24:5-7 - *"The earth is also defiled under its inhabitants, because they **have transgressed the laws, violated the statutes, and broken the everlasting covenant**.*

Therefore the curse has devoured the earth, and those who dwell in it are desolate. Therefore the inhabitants of the earth are burned, and few men are left.

6) Because they believe in many gods.

Is. 44:6 - *"Thus says the Lord, the King of Israel, And his Redeemer, the Lord of hosts: 'I am the First and I am the Last; **Besides Me there is no God**."*

Is. 45:6 - *"That they may know from the rising of the*

sun to its setting That there is none besides Me. I am the Lord, and there is no other;"

2) Because they deny their creator:

Is. 29:16 - they deny the maker; they replace Him with false gods and doctrines (like evolution). **(Is. 45:9; Rom. 9:20)**

3) Many have forsaken God and have instead chosen the prince of this world (Satan):

Is. 28:15; Ezek. 13:22 - *"they have made a covenant with death; with sheol they are in agreement"*

4) *There will soon come a time when* the cup of iniquity will become full and overflows; this is when the Great Tribulation and the "Great day of God Almighty" the Battle of Armageddon begins (**Rev. 16:14-16**)
Joel 3:13 - *"Put in the sickle, for the harvest is ripe. Come, go down; for the winepress is full, the vats overflow— for their wickedness is great."*

5) God knows that fallen man requires judgment before he or she repents:

Isaiah 26:9 *". . . for when thy judgments are in the earth, the inhabitants of the world will learn righteousness."*

Mankind will either learn righteousness by practicing it

or by experiencing it. The later has become society's

choice, and that is God's reason for the coming judgments. The following verse reveals that the earth is judged because of its iniquity. Let's read:

Is 24:5-6 *"The earth is polluted because of its inhabitants, because they have transgressed the laws, violated the statutes, and broken the everlasting covenant. Therefore a curse devours the earth, and those who dwell in it are desolate. Therefore the inhabitants of the earth are burned, and few men are left."*

7) Because many will accept the Mark of the Beast during the Apocalypse

Although it may be hard to believe it at this time, the prophecies reveal that at the time of the end the inhabitants of the world will be so demon possessed, and unfamiliar with the word of God that they will choose to take the mark of the beast as prophesied in **Revelation 13**. Why would anyone take the mark of the beast (**666**) when it will damn them forever? Because they do not believe the words of God and they would rather believe the lies of Satan, and to continue to live in sin. Their lack of faith and knowledge will also blind them to the truth. Let's read some of the passages that reveal this:

Dan. 12:10 - *"Many shall be purified, made white, and refined, but the wicked shall do wickedly; and **none of the wicked shall understand**, but the wise shall understand."*

Hosea 4:6 - *"**My people are destroyed for lack of knowledge**. Because **you have rejected knowledge**, I also will reject you from being priests for Me; because you have forgotten the law of your God, I also will forget your children."*

1 Cor. 1:18-19 - *"For **the message of the cross is foolishness to those who are perishing**, but to us who are being saved it is the power of God. For it is written: "**I will destroy the wisdom of the wise**, and bring to nothing the understanding of the prudent."* **Is. 29-14**

Note: This explains why so many folks have a hard time accepting Jesus Christ as Lord and savior and why so many consider God's elect as foolish for believing in Christ.

2nd Thessalonians 2:11 - *"And for this reason **God will send them strong delusion, that they should believe the lie**." **Rom. 1:28***

Satan is spewing many lies (through our world leaders, and the media) in these end times, and since many are already deluded due to their lack of faith and knowledge of the word, many believe the lies of this world which is influenced by the devil. Also, since many folks don't even believe that Satan or God exist they have no choice but believe in anything that sounds rational, and therefore they will accept any solution that comes their way including a mark (666) that will allow them to buy and sell during the apocalypse (which will give them just a bit more time before they suffer much greater consequences than those who refuse the mark - allegiance with Satan)! Imagine how much worse it will get once the restrainer, and God's veil of protection is removed from this world; actually the next section reveals how bad it will get.

Proof # 100 - The Bible Reveals how this age will end.

No other religion and no other book, provides such a clear and unequivocal description on how this age will conclude. The following prophecies have withstood the test of time - given that no other religion, person or god has been able to suppress or contest these prophecies. This alone should offer ample proof to the skeptics that the words of the bible are divinely inspired.

It is clear that at the time of the end, this age will conclude with a massive **earthquake and fire**. Below are just 2 of many prophecies that reveal this age will conclude with a massive earthquake and fire:

Rev. 16:18-21 *"And there were noises and thundering and lightning; and **there was a great earthquake, such a mighty and great earthquake as had not occurred since men were on the earth**. Now the great city was divided into three parts, and **the cities of the nations fell**. And great Babylon was remembered before God, to give her the cup of the wine of the fierceness of His wrath. Then **every island fled away, and the mountains were not found**. And **great hail from heaven** fell upon men, each hailstone about the weight of a talent. Men* blasphemed God because of the plague of the hail, since that plague was exceedingly great."

<u>Micah 1:4</u> - *"The **mountains will melt** under Him, and the valleys will split like wax before the fire, like waters poured down a steep place."*

<u>Zechariah 14:12</u> - *"And this shall be the plague with which the Lord will strike all the people who fought against Jerusalem: their flesh shall dissolve while they stand on their feet, their eyes shall dissolve in their sockets, and their tongues shall dissolve in their mouths."*

<u>Is 24:5-7</u> - *"The earth is also defiled under its inhabitants, because they **have transgressed the laws, violated the statutes, and broken the everlasting covenant**.*

Therefore the curse has devoured the earth, and those who dwell in it are desolate. Therefore the inhabitants of the earth are burned, and few men are left.

If you are interested in learning more about the coming apocalypse, you may want to grab a copy of the following book(s) all by Robert Rite:

Signs in the Heavens
Revelation Mysteries Decoded
Blood Moons Rising
Apocalypse Countdown 2015 to 2021

Chapter 14 - The Secret of the Prophecies

The last book of the bible is called the **Revelation of Jesus Christ.** The secret of the prophecies is that they all point to Jesus Christ as the Messiah and the King of Heaven, as revealed by His angel:

*"Then he said to me, "Write: 'Blessed are those who are called to the **marriage supper of the Lamb**!'" And he said to me, "These are the true sayings of God." And I fell at his feet to worship him. But he said to me, "See that you do not do that! I am your fellow servant, and of your brethren who have the testimony of Jesus. Worship God! For **the testimony of Jesus is the spirit of prophecy**."* **Revelation 19:9-10**

There is none other

Many may wonder why would the God of the universe care so much about tiny Israel or this tiny planet earth. Instead of glorifying omnipotent God for the creation of this mind boggling expanse called the universe, many have been misled into believing that one God could not have possibly created so much. They in essence prefer to embrace false doctrines that claim that there are many gods, and many ways to God, which of course they cannot prove because it is not true!

This is clearly contrary to what the God of the bible declares; that there is only one God; only ONE creator of the universe:

Isaiah 44:6 *"Thus says the Lord, the King of Israel, And his Redeemer, the Lord of hosts: 'I am the First and I am the Last;* **Besides Me there is no God.***"*

Isaiah 44:24: *"Thus says the Lord, you're Redeemer, and He who formed you from the womb:*
"I am the Lord, who makes all things, who **stretches out the heavens all alone***, who spreads abroad the earth* **by Myself***;"*

A war wearied world still hopes for peace

After six thousand years of relentless wars, mankind still believes that peace without the **Prince of Peace** can be a reality. Well we have clearly seen how it will not become a reality until the Messiah returns to establish His kingdom here on earth.

Jeremiah 9:8 - *"Their tongue is an arrow shot out; it speaks deceit; one* **speaks peaceably to his neighbor with his mouth, but in his heart he lies in wait***."*

As we discussed, all the false peace agreements between Israel and its neighbors have only led to increased instability and violence in the Middle East region.

Knowledge vs. Wisdom

How unfortunate that mankind, including the highly educated, place so much value and trust on carnal knowledge and yet are blinded to the truth as revealed by the word of God. They substitute carnal knowledge for heavenly knowledge (wisdom) which

God bestows upon those that place their trust on Him. Remember that every theory formed by the carnal mind (that is not scriptural) is under the influence of the **prince** of this world - and therefore will most likely contradict or distort the word of God.

God has demonstrated here on earth how he can do so much with so little - a testament to His glory. The tiny nation of Israel (God's Land) and tiny planet earth (in comparison to the Universe) are clear examples of this. Yet I believe that tiny Israel and tiny earth are just the beginnings of God's plan for His elect through eternity.

A universe that is barren, lifeless and beckoning for life clearly indicate that God is only just beginning in expanding His creative mastery through infinity! No doubt that his elect will play a role in executing His glory in the unending expanse.

God's Number 7

In an earlier chapter we learned that God's glory is even revealed in numbers; primarily the number seven.

Indeed God's total plan for mankind revolves around the number seven. And the significance of this number is not just for Israel but for all mankind. Seven is God's number of completion, and the seventh number is Holy (i.e. the Sabbath day of rest). God made us in his image - God is Holy! **Genesis 1:26. The number seven is indeed the number of God**. The number seven stands for eternity and it is our destiny for those who choose to be Holy children of God through perpetuity!

You have been called for this time!

As Mordecai told Esther - you have been called for this time!

"For if you remain completely silent at this time, relief

and deliverance will arise for the Jews from another place, but you and your father's house will perish......"
Esther 4:14

The above passage applied to Israel and applies to us today. ***There will come a time soon when we will have to stand up for the Lord despite the consequences***. The world is blind to what is coming - but now you know.

The Lord has promised that He will hasten all these things, in its time. (**Is. 60:22**)

You can be sheltered on the coming Day of the Lord

There is a way for us to be sheltered during the coming apocalypse and the key word here is humility. Let's read:

Zephaniah 2:3 - *"Seek the Lord, all you humble of the earth, who have upheld His justice. Seek righteousness, seek humility. It may be that you will be hidden in the day of the Lord's anger."*

I have set before you over 100 proofs that the bible is the inspired word of God. Now it all boils down to one

choice for you. Are you to place your trust

and faith in the created or the creator? That is the

challenge for humanity in these last days.

It is time to decide whether the 100 plus proofs that I have set forth for you herewith are sufficient for you to make the right decision. As Moses proclaimed before the children of Israel:

*"I call heaven and earth as witnesses today against you, that **I have set before you life and death**, **blessing and cursing**; therefore **choose life**, that both you and your descendants may live;"*

Your fellow servant signs out.

Get Complimentary Access to: "Prophecy Alerts"

Dear Reader: Prophecies are being fulfilled so rapidly in these last days that I am offering my readers complimentary access to "***prophecy alerts***" so that you get "***Breaking Prophecy News***" as soon as it breaks...Just follow this link below and sign Up today...
http://robertritebooks.com/prophecy-alerts/

About Robert Rite

Robert Rite is the author of over 18 books including:

- "Apocalypse Countdown - 2015 to 2021"
- "Apocalypse Codes - Decoding the Prophecies in the Book of Daniel"
- "100 Proofs that the Bible is the Inspired Word of God and Scientifically Accurate"
- "Ancient Apocalypse Codes"
- "Awaken the Supernatural You!"
- "Aliens, Fallen Angels, Nephilim and the Supernatural"
- "Babylon the Great is Fallen, is Fallen! Who is "Mystery Babylon" of the End of Days?"
- "Blood Moons Rising"
- "Be healed!....How to Unlock the Supernatural Healing Power of God"
- "Bible Verses for Supernatural Blessings"
- End of Days
- "God, Mystery Religions, Cults, and the coming Global Religion"
- "Prophecies of the Apocalypse: Unlocking the End Time Prophetic Codes as Revealed by the Ancient Prophets"
- "Revelation Mysteries Decoded: Unlocking the Secrets of the coming Apocalypse"
- "Signs in the Heavens, Divine Secrets of the Zodiac & the Blood Moons of 2014!"
- "The New Age Movement vs. Christianity: and the Coming Global Religion"
- "Unlocking the Supernatural Power of Prayer"
- "128 Powerful Bible Verses that can Save Your Life!"

Robert is also the creator of over 135 articles on bible facts, and end-of-day mysteries and prophecies among other related topics. Visit Robert at RobertRiteBooks.com for sample chapters, press releases and related information.

Says Robert Rite:

"It is said that the truth at times is more stimulating than fiction. So have the best of both worlds, and stimulate your mind and soul with subject matter - that really matters"

Robert Rite - Social Profiles:
Blog URLs:
http://RobertRiteBooks.com

Amazon Author Page: http://www.amazon.com/-/e/B00GOGIBEG

Facebook Page:
https://www.facebook.com/robertritebooks
Robert Rite at Twitter
Twitter Handle: @robertrite
You Tube Channel:
https://www.youtube.com/channel/UCbED4FN2Pww-u-o1uO0qylQ
Google Plus URL:
https://plus.google.com/u/0/100112453810665259776/posts/p/pub
LinkedIn:
https://www.linkedin.com/profile/preview?locale=en_US&trk=prof-0-sb-preview-primary-button
Pinterest:
http://www.pinterest.com/frontierins/
Stumble Upon:
http://www.stumbleupon.com/stumbler/RobertRite

Instagram: https://instagram.com/robertrite/

Credits and Recommended reading:

Douglas, Brooks (2011-12-03). Proof That The Bible Is True (Kindle Locations 268-273). Victory Baptist Press. Kindle Edition.
The Incomplete Church by Sid Roth
http://www. matthewmcgee.org/evidence.html
mysteryoftheinquity. wordpress.com
Source: Young Islands, Canyons, and Dinosaurs - www. khouse.org
Darwin's Enigma - Luther D. Sunderland
The Incredible Human Potential - Herbert W. Armstrong
Young Islands, Canyons, and Dinosaurs - www. khouse.org
http://www. dcclothesline.com/2014/01/09/44-reasons-evolution-just-fairy-tale-adults/
Perry Stone - Mana Fest 2015
http://endoftheamericandream. com/archives/why-are-giant-sinkholes-appearing-all-over-america-is-something-happening-to-the-earths-crust
- Why the Big Bang is a fizzle and stars cannot evolve out of gas; By Kent R. Rieske, Biblelife

www.ingramcontent.com/pod-product-compliance
Lightning Source LLC
Chambersburg PA
CBHW060505030426

42337CB00015B/1740